# PEARLS *of* WISDOM

# PEARLS

*of*

# WISDOM

## 30 Inspirational Ideas
## to Live Your Best Life Now!

## JACK CANFIELD

### MARCI SHIMOFF

### JANET BRAY ATTWOOD

### CHRIS ATTWOOD

Allison Jacob, Editor
Text design by Jane Hagaman

Hierophant Publishing
www.hierophantpublishing.com
www.pearlsofwisdomthebook.com

If you are unable to order this book from your local
bookseller, you may order directly from the publisher.

Library of Congress Control Number: 2011941640

ISBN 978-0-9818771-5-0
10 9 8 7 6 5 4 3 2 1

Printed on acid-free paper in the United States

# Contents

# Publisher's Statement

*Pearls of Wisdom: 30 Inspirational Ideas to Live Your Best Life Now!* is a treasure trove of wisdom and advice from some of the most well-known self-help authors and the best new self-help authors in the genre today.

These gurus of metamorphosis have each written a chapter based on personal experience that present a transformational idea to improve your life, now! There is great diversity in the chapters, ranging from the cerebral (such as recognizing the fractal patterns in our lives) to the practical (the importance of relaxation and meditation instructions), and they will inspire you on the road to success while reminding you to love yourself throughout the journey.

The ideas in *Pearls of Wisdom* are designed to offer keys for each of the many doors that block the road to your best life, and our sincere hope is that by implementing some, if not all, of these wonderful ideas, you will alter your life in truly meaningful ways and reveal the pearl that is inside you.

*Sincerely,*
*The Hierophant Editorial Staff*

# Inspired Action Gets It Done

## by Jack Canfield

I have had an enormous amount of success in my life, and I owe it all to two things. The first is that I have learned how to access my intuition and tune in to my inner guidance (which comes from both my own subconscious mind and from God); I have learned how to meditate, use guided visualization, and read the kinesthetic signals from my body (what some people call learning to trust your gut). The second is that I have learned to quickly act on my inner guidance—the sooner the better!

## The Power of Asking for Inner Guidance

Asking for inner guidance through meditation has provided me with some very powerful ideas, ones that have accelerated the rate and magnified the size of my personal and professional success. When we needed a title for the book of inspirational and motivational stories that Mark Victor Hansen and I had compiled, I agreed to meditate an hour a day in search of the perfect title. I simply asked God to give me a title, then I sat in silence waiting for it. Nothing emerged the first two days, but on the third day, a green chalk board, like the ones used in schools, suddenly emerged. Then a hand appeared and wrote the words "Chicken Soup" on the board. I contemplated that for a moment, then I asked what I assumed was God's hand: "What does chicken soup have to do with this book?"

I heard, "Your grandmother used to give you chicken soup when you were sick as a kid."

I replied, "But this book isn't about sick people."

The voice responded, "People's spirits are sick."

This was in 1992 during the recession that accompanied the first Gulf War, and many people were indeed living in fear, hopelessness, and resignation.

I played with the title "Chicken Soup for the Spirit," which didn't sound quite right, and then it morphed into "Chicken Soup for the Soul" . . . and I immediately got goose bumps—what Mark likes to call God bumps. They almost always seem to accompany an idea that is deeply aligned with what is for my highest good.

I immediately got up from meditation and told my wife, who got goose bumps. Then I called Mark, who got goose bumps, and our agent, who also got goose bumps. By the end of the day the full title had emerged—*Chicken Soup for the Soul: 101 Stories to Open the Heart and Rekindle the Spirit.* It seemed we were definitely onto something.

## Inspiration Must Be Followed by Action

Sometimes inspirations occur without our even seeming to ask for them. Other times, we have to ask for them, then create the quiet space within which to receive them. They can occur while lying in bed in a semiconscious dream state, while taking a shower, or while walking along a beach or through the woods. But however and whenever they come, they need to be acted on as soon as possible. I have come to believe that when they come, they come in a certain window of time that is ideally suited for the action to begin at that moment.

So Mark, our agent, and I headed off to New York City to sell our book. Unfortunately, during the three days we were in New York City, no one at the fifteen publishing houses we visited got goose bumps. Everyone told us that nobody bought collections of short stories and that our title was stupid. Our agent became so discouraged that he gave us the book back and said he could not sell it.

## Action Must Be Consistent and Persistent

That is when we had to choose between believing in our dream and trusting our inner guidance or believing the naysayers in the publishing industry and trusting their judgments. Well, one of the secrets of success that I have learned is to never give up on the dreams that come from deep in your heart. In fact, by this time, our dream had become more of a divine obsession. We couldn't let it go. So we took more action. Over the next five months, we were rejected by 144 publishers. Eventually, we went to the American Booksellers Association Convention and walked the floor of the exhibit area for three days asking hundreds of publishers, "Will you publish our book?" It was not until late in the third day that Health Communications, Inc., a little publisher in Deerfield Beach, Florida, decided to seriously look at our book. A month later they decided to publish it.

## The Rule of Five

When the book finally came out in July 1993, it was not an overnight success. It wasn't until a year later that it hit its first bestsellers list. But it was during that year that Mark and I came up with what we dubbed the Rule of Five. We agreed to take five action steps every single day, except on holidays and vacations, to promote and sell our book. One day, we called five radio stations and asked them to interview us about the book. On another, we sent out five free review copies to book reviewers and influential people. One of those people was the producer of the hit television show *Touched by an Angel*. She was so taken by the book that she required all of her writers, directors, cameramen, and other crew members to read the book. She said that the feelings generated and evoked by our stories were the same ones she wanted to create in their TV episodes. That story made it into *Variety* and later onto the Associated Press wire and generated thousands of book sales. We also bought the book *1001 Ways to Market Your Book,* by John Kremer, and wrote each way on a Post-it note and stuck them all on a long wall in our office. We did five of those suggestions every day. Eventually, *Chicken Soup for the Soul* reached number one on the *New York Times* list and stayed there for almost three years, selling ten million copies along the way.

Stop for a moment and ask yourself, "What are the five action steps that I need to take every day—no matter what—to achieve my number one goal?" If your top goal is to lose fifty pounds, it might be: 1) do some form of aerobic exercise for forty-five minutes; 2) drink ten glasses of water a day; 3) lift weights for fifteen minutes; 4) meditate for fifteen minutes; and 5) read something or listen to a CD about motivation or weight loss for fifteen minutes. Other options are do not eat dessert, do not eat sugar, cut out all fast-burning carbohydrates, take a walk after dinner, and get eight hours of sleep. In this case, you would do the same five things, or a combination from a list of ten things, every single day.

The Rule of Five can also be applied to your professional goals. One example is the Keller-Williams's 5-10-15-5 formula. They swear that anyone who uses this formula will have success in real estate sales. Have five in-person meetings with potential property listers or potential buyers. Have ten telephone conversations. Send out fifteen thank-you cards to the people you met with. Then go view five properties that are for sale so that you are very familiar with the inventory available. Everyone I know in real estate sales who follows this formula has indeed been very successful.

## Not All Actions Produce
## Instant or Perfect Results

Not everything you try is going to work. Remember the Law of Probabilities, which states that the more things you try, the more likely one of them will work; the more books you read, the more likely one of them will change your life; the more people you meet, the more likely one of them will have the answer or be the relationship you are looking for.

## Solicit and Respond to Feedback

To keep moving forward toward your dreams and goals, pay attention to the feedback you receive and adjust accordingly. Positive feedback consists of good health, many good friends, lots of sales, plenty of money, fun, joy, and happiness. Negative feedback consists of ill health, physical pain, few friends, few sales, no job, debt, constant anger, and depression. All these negatives tell you that you are not thinking the right thoughts, visualizing the right images, or taking the right actions. Pay attention. Don't go into denial. Face up to what isn't working.

The fastest way to accelerate your success is to ask for feedback from as many people as possible, thank them for it, and act on as much of it as makes sense. Here is a very powerful question for soliciting useful feedback that I learned from Strategic Coach Dan Sullivan.

> On a scale of 1 to 10, how would you rate the quality of (our product, my service, the installation, me as a parent, me as a spouse, me as an employee, etc.) this past week/month?

Anything less than a 10, gets this follow-up question: What would it take to make it a 10?

It is in the answer to this last question that all the valuable information lies. Have the courage to ask this question of everyone you interact with on a regular basis. No matter how painful or discomforting their answer is, say, "Thank you for caring enough to share that with me." Don't argue with them. Just take in the feedback, see if it fits, and experiment with trying on some new behaviors.

## Perseverance

Finally, never give up. Make corrections based on feedback so that you are constantly improving and getting better, but don't give up. If we had stopped trying to sell the first *Chicken Soup for the Soul* book after one hundred rejections, I would not be sitting here writing this today. If we had stopped trying to promote, market, and sell the book after six months of no major results, I would not be a multimillionaire who has traveled to more than forty countries speaking and training people on the principles contained in that book and my other books.

It has taken more than fifteen years to build a brand that has generated more than a billion dollars in retail sales and has created more than twenty licensed products, including Chicken Soup for the Pet Lovers Soul dog and cat foods. So also be patient.

If you follow your heart, believe in your dreams, trust your inner guidance, take action, solicit and respond to feedback, and persevere no matter what, you will eventually find yourself living a life far greater than you ever could have imagined.

JACK CANFIELD is the co-creator and coauthor of the *New York Times* bestselling *Chicken Soup for the Soul* book series, which has sold more than 500 million books in forty-seven languages, and *The Success Principles: How to Get from Where You Are to Where You Want to Be.* He has appeared in eight films, including *The Secret, The Truth, Tapping the Source,* and *Discover the Gift.* He is the CEO of the Canfield Training Group in Santa Barbara, California, and is a much sought-after speaker who conducts transformational trainings and delivers dynamic keynote speeches all across the world.

You can find out more about him and his work at
www.JackCanfield.com.

# The Secret to Living a Passionate Life

## By Janet Bray Attwood and Chris Attwood

Most people know that passion is common to all successful people. The power of the Passion Test lies in the fact that now, for the first time, discovering your passions is not hit or miss. Passion is no longer something available to only the lucky few.

Through a simple yet powerful process, anyone can discover the things that matter most to them in their lives.

But the question then remains, is that enough to be successful?

The answer is no.

What distinguishes those who have enjoyed enduring success in their fields from everyone else is that they have learned to make their passions the basis of every significant decision in their lives. As we say in our book *The Passion Test:* "Whenever you are faced with a choice, a decision, or an opportunity, choose in favor of your passions."

This is what we call the "secret that guarantees a passionate life."

Like most fundamental truths, it's easy to say but more challenging to put into practice. Why? Because when you are faced with important decisions, rarely will you know what the outcome will be, and often it will appear that choosing in favor of your passions could lead to disaster.

Because of this, there is one crucial quality that anyone who wants to live a happy, joyful, fulfilling, and successful life has to develop: trust.

Trust grows as you come to realize that it's not an accident that you love the things you do. Those things, those passions, exist because they are what will lead you to fulfill your purpose for being alive. When your life is connected to those passions, it feels meaningful, and when your life has meaning, it is fulfilling.

Ultimately, living a joy-filled life means coming to trust that life is beneficent. That means every experience, every person, every situation in your life is there to help you open up to the fullest possible experience of yourself and your life.

Choosing in favor of your passions is the key to success in life, but is it scary? You bet! Especially when everyone around you is saying that you can't do it, it won't work, you're being crazy, etc. And take our word for it, you're not alone. *All* successful people have those naysayers in their lives.

Janet chose in favor of her passion to become a transformational leader when she made the decision to leave her position as director of marketing at Books Are Fun, the third largest book buyer in the U.S., to partner with Mark Victor Hansen and Robert Allen. She left a comfortable, six-figure income with benefits to step into a role with no guaranteed income and no idea whether she could do what was needed.

Did that take courage? Absolutely.

How did it turn out?

Ten years later, Janet is a *New York Times* bestselling author, she travels around the world sharing her passion and her love, and she runs her own multi-million-dollar business.

But what if she had stayed at Books Are Fun?

Over the past ten years, the company was sold to *Reader's Digest,* which then went through some hard times, and the new company dwindled dramatically in size. If Janet had stayed there, the odds are she would have ended up being laid off just like most of the other employees that she had worked with.

You can't know how things will turn out when you choose in favor of your passions. That's why it takes courage to make those choices. But as you begin to make them, you will start to discover how the miraculous becomes a regular part of your own life.

When Chris married a beautiful German woman in 2006, his new wife told him, "It's really important to me that we spend at least four to six months a year in Europe."

Now, if Chris hadn't been clear about his passions, this could have been an impossible choice. He could either go with his wife to Europe and risk losing all of his income-producing activities in the U.S., or he could stay in the U.S. and risk losing his wife.

What kind of choice is that?

But Chris takes the Passion Test regularly and was completely clear about his top five passions. While his business activities were on that list, spending time with his new wife was the priority. So, when his wife told him this, his immediate response was: "Of course we'll do that."

In the first year of their marriage, Chris and Doe spent a month in the Canary Islands, two months in Switzerland, and several months in Germany. They had a fabulous time.

Did Chris give up his love for his business activities? No. But he rearranged his schedule to spend time with his family in the mornings, then work in the afternoon and evening when he could connect with people in the U.S.

Interestingly, during that year, the business did better than it ever had, and since then, the business has continued to grow, in spite of the fact that Chris will spend almost nine months in Europe this year.

Could he have known this would be the outcome ahead of time? No.

And you won't know your outcomes, either. When it's time to choose in favor of your passions, you are going to be forced to trust that things will work out okay.

Our suggestion is to take baby steps every day in the direction of the things you love.

If your life is financially on the edge, don't jump off of a cliff into a completely new world to start a whole new life. Don't uproot your whole family or quit your only source of income to follow your passions until you've had some experience making those choices and seeing how things work out. As you consistently choose in favor the things that have greatest meaning for you, the people, the places, and the things that you need will show up to support you in living your passionate life.

"What you love and God's will for you is one and the same." What this means is that the universe doesn't play tricks. It's not a mistake that you love the things you do. By consistently choosing in favor of your passions, you will find that you will naturally have the courage you need to live a fulfilled, successful life, one step or one huge leap at a time. As you grow in trust, more and more you'll find that you are able to say yes to bigger and greater passions.

So next time you're faced with an important

decision, ask yourself, "Will making this choice help me be more connected to the things I love and care about, or will it take me farther away from them?" If the answer is closer, then say yes.

You'll be pleasantly surprised by the results.

And remember, "What you love and God's will for you is one and the same."

JANET BRAY ATTWOOD AND CHRIS ATTWOOD are coauthors of the *New York Times* bestseller *The Passion Test: The Effortless Path to Discovering Your Life Purpose.* Their company, Enlightened Alliances, arranged 70 percent of the interviews for the movie and book, *The Secret.*

Janet speaks throughout the world on how to discover passion and purpose and has shared the stage with His Holiness the 14th Dalai Lama, Dr. Stephen Covey, Richard Branson, Nobel Peace Prize–winner F. W. de Klerk, Jack Canfield, Zappos.com CEO Tony Hsieh, Rev. Michael Beckwith, and many others.

Janet and Chris are founding members of the Transformational Leadership Council, a group of more than one hundred of the top speakers and authors in the world. They are also co-founders of the Passion Test Daily, an online magazine, and the Transformational Magazine Network.

The purpose of their Passion Test Programs is to "Inspire Transformation through Love," and they are living examples of the power of love. Though they were once married but no longer are, they continue to be best friends and business partners. After Chris remarried in 2006, he and his wife asked Janet to be godmother to their two daughters.

# How to Activate Self-Love in Your Life

## by Marci Shimoff

*Whatever you are doing, love yourself for doing it.*
*Whatever you are feeling, love yourself for feeling it.*
—Thaddeus Golas, twentieth-century
author and philosopher

The year was 1971, and "hot pants" were all the rage. In case you weren't around for that particular fashion flurry, hot pants were three-inch-long shorts, usually in wild psychedelic colors and patterns, that barely covered your butt.

I was thirteen years old at the time, and the fact

that my nickname was "Chubs" didn't stop me from squeezing into my very own pair of bright pink hot pants. All the girls in my school were wearing them and—no surprise—I wanted to be one of the crowd.

The day of my hot pants debut, I walked home from school with my best friend, Chris. At my house, we decided to call our other friend, Roselyn, for a good old "who-likes-who/he-said-she-said" teenage gossip session. Chris dialed the number from the kitchen phone, and I went to my bedroom to use the extension there. As I picked up the receiver, I heard Roselyn say, "Can you *believe* Marci wore *hot pants* today—with *those* thighs?"

My face burning with shame, I silently put down the receiver. I took off the tiny pink shorts and stuck them at the very back of my closet where I would never have to see them again.

But I couldn't get rid of Roselyn's voice as easily. Every time I looked into the mirror, I heard, "Can you *believe* how fat you are?" Later, when I was nineteen and didn't have a boyfriend, that same voice asked, "Can you *believe* what a loser you are?" And years after that, when I gave a talk and thought someone in the audience looked bored, the voice was still there: "Can you *believe* what a lousy speaker you are?"

It took years for me to hang up the phone on my inner critic. She was successfully employed full-time, pointing out every "unlovable" part of myself and keeping me from feeling unconditional love for myself.

If you're like everyone else I've ever met, you have the equivalent of a "hot pants" story in your life and your own version of self-judgment, both of which have put a lid on your experience of love and happiness.

Decades after this hot pants incident, I felt compelled to explore whether it was possible to experience unconditional love for ourselves and for everyone else. Could I actually love myself no matter what?

I had spent years studying and teaching self-esteem, and I'd realized that there's a big difference between self-esteem and self-love. Self-esteem is based on "loving myself, because . . ." I'll love myself if I'm good enough, smart enough, pretty enough, do a good enough job, and so on. This is what I call "love for good reason," and the limitations of this are clear. What happens when I don't live up to the exacting standards that I hold? Then I plunge into self-judgment, close my heart, and feel unworthy of love. Not a great recipe for a happy life.

We place these same kinds of conditions on our love for other people, as well. We'll love them if we approve of them, agree with them, or share our values with them. If they don't meet our requirements, then we shut down love.

There is an alternative—what I call "love for no reason." This is the basis for true self-love and love for others. It's an unconditional love that doesn't depend on our behavior or on any other person or situation having to be a particular way. It's a state of being that we bring to all of our experiences, rather than try to "get" from the world around us.

I set out to find out how to live in this state, and the answers eventually led me to write *Love for No Reason: 7 Steps to Creating a Life of Unconditional Love.* I took the same approach I had for my earlier book, *Happy for No Reason,* in which I interviewed unconditionally happy people to find out how to be truly happy. This time, I went to the experts on love— more than 150 people whom I call "Love Luminaries," including scientists, psychologists, spiritual teachers, and people whose lives were rich in the qualities of the heart—to find out how to live in a state of unconditional love.

My research bore great news—we can definitely grow in unconditional love for ourselves and for others, but it takes practice to reverse some old habits. Since most of us are trained to base our love on reasons, we have some undoing to do. By understanding that there is a love that goes beyond reasons, you've made the first step.

Here are three simple practices that can help you love yourself no matter what. These are especially useful when you're having a rough time or being particularly judgmental with yourself.

**1. Practice self-care:** Most people aren't in the habit of taking good care of themselves and honoring their own needs. Luckily, beginning that process is actually quite simple: you start by becoming aware of those needs. Three times a day, stop what you're doing and ask yourself, *What's the most loving thing I can do for myself right now?* Then pay very close attention to the answer.

Sometimes the most loving thing you can do for yourself in the moment is to drink a glass of water or to walk outside and get some fresh air. Other times, it may be to clean out your email inbox so you feel less stressed or to call a good friend to get some support. The important thing is to make that question a part of your daily practice and then follow through with action.

**2. Practice self-compassion and forgiveness:** It can be far more difficult to forgive ourselves than it is to forgive others. We often give others the benefit of the doubt that we don't give to ourselves. Developing self-love requires that you treat yourself kindly—as kindly as you would your neighbor or your friend.

If you're stuck in self-criticism, try thinking of yourself as a completely separate person. Ask yourself, *What would I do if I saw a friend hurting the way that I am hurting?* This gentle approach is actually more effective for moving forward in life and "righting the wrongs" we're beating ourselves up for. Who has more energy—a discouraged, dejected person or a supported and loved one? Give yourself all the benefits of having a good friend—from the inside out.

**3. Practice self-expression:** Expressing yourself builds on the first practice: self-care. You can only express your needs and wants when you know what they are yourself. Once you know, the next step is to communicate them to others simply and clearly. For a lot of us, this is scary. The secret is to start small. Each day for the next month, ask for something or express yourself in a way that stretches you slightly but doesn't feel impossible. Each time you practice this, you're strengthening the neural pathways in your brain that support self-love.

As you do these practices, you may wonder whether you are being selfish—far from it! Growing in self-love is one of the most generous things you can do. Because our emotions are contagious, when you love and care for yourself, others around you *catch* your love. And isn't a world filled with love the kind we all want to live in?

MARCI SHIMOFF is a renowned motivational speaker and a *New York Times* bestselling author of *Love for No Reason: 7 Steps to Creating a Life of Unconditional Love* (Free Press, December 2010). *Love for No Reason* offers a breakthrough approach to experiencing a lasting state of unconditional love—the kind of love that doesn't depend on another person, situation, or romantic partner and that you can access at any time and in any circumstance. This is the key to lasting joy and fulfillment in life.

Visit www.TheLoveBook.com for more information.
Follow Marci on Facebook at MarciShimoffFan.

# Change Your Story, Change Your Life

## by Barnet Bain

Once upon a time, in a land before social networks, smart phones, gaming, iPads, and a gazillion TV channel universes, the primary story experience was still hooked up to family life. As a boy, the stories I heard around our dining room table defined how I saw myself.

Family narratives used to reveal how and where we fit into the bigger picture. They pointed the way to vital traditions of connection and meaning. Stories have always been the glue of community life. It has been that way in every culture.

Until now.

Now family time has been replaced by media time. Modern stories arrive one size fits all, products for a consumer culture. By the time a child turns ten years old, he or she has an imagination structured by tens of thousands of messages, all reinforcing the whopper that meaning can be found through the brand of running shoes you wear or the kind of ride you drive.

As a result, separation and alienation have never been greater.

When I was still a newcomer to the film industry and fighting for my place at the table, I complained one night to an old mentor about the harsh unfairness of Hollywood. He was not buying a word of it.

"You are forgetting, Barnet. You are not in Hollywood. Hollywood is *in you.*"

I chewed on that one for a long time before the light went on.

Nowadays I am being bombarded with information from a variety of sources. I have had to become a conscious story consumer. I am responsible for every message I let in from a story. It is up to me to participate.

There has to be a contract between an audience

and a storyteller for the magic to occur. It is a cocreation. Walt Whitman said, "To have great poets, there must be great audiences." If we don't know what value to expect from the contract, then maybe it is because we have lost sight of our roles as participants.

Quantum physics tells us that an observer has something to do with the experience of reality. If the environment is an extension of my mind, even a little, then if I change my mind about what is important to me, it will produce different results.

In other words, if you change your story, you will change your life. There are no bystanders in the commerce of stories. *We are all participants.*

Here are some ways I approach it.

From action-hero stories, I get what it means to live every moment as if it were my last. I'm engaged, involved, and committed to a cause. I participate with honor. I understand the importance of "get up and go."

Love stories unfold in enchanted pockets of gracious giving and receiving. They foster my compassion for the loss and hurts of others: physical, emotional, mental, and spiritual. They tease open my heart and mind.

Space operas and science fiction help me see past the world of form. Beneath the veneer of every alien civilization and dimension await shared universal tests. How do I make a difference? Live more. Stretch more. Forgive more. What am I prepared to move beyond (or leave behind) to access the Force within, to go boldly into the unknown?

Dramatic stories help me connect with the feelings of others and how I deal with my own relationships with my spouse, children, friends, boss, colleagues, myself, Higher Self, and God/Goddess/All That Is. When I can recognize myself in another person, it increases my ability to respond to them and their situations.

Comedies always force me to wonder why I take myself so seriously. Funny stories remind me to laugh, to find humor in the frantic dance I do for love without remembering I am loved all along.

Horror stories and war stories have lots to reveal about what is dark in me as well as what is light. They often reflect judgments or emotions that are not fully expressed or that I am denying altogether. Stories that arouse strong feelings of antipathy in me are always a sure sign of resistances, fears, and blockages to my growth that persist below the waterline of my awareness. What I resist persists.

We can change our stories as easy as this. Somehow the world magically rearranges itself to reflect a new story. Take a moment to experiment for yourself. Pick a story, event, or conversation, and start with these steps.

- ❖ What is your reaction to the so-called facts of your current story? Does it make you angry? Does it upset you? Do you wish it would go away?

- ❖ Create an alternative meaning for your story, one that you prefer. But no super heroes or helpful aliens. It must be within your realm of possibility. You are the protagonist; you are the hero.

- ❖ Feed your new story with committed attention and be vigilant for evidence to support it.

- ❖ Stay detached from any messages to the contrary. Don't let them suck you in.

- ❖ Most importantly, live your new story as your highest truth.

If you practice this, you will be actively aligning yourself with principles of quantum creativity where, by simply changing your story, you can create powerful changes in your life.

BARNET BAIN is a "creativity doctor" and coach. He is an award-winning producer and director of numerous films, including Emmy-nominated *Homeless to Harvard*, Oscar winner *What Dreams May Come, The Celestine Prophecy,* and *The Lost and Found Family.* Barnet can be heard as co-host of Cutting Edge Consciousness radio on KKZZ AM Southern California and in podcasts from Changing Times Media (www.cuttingedgeconsciousness.com). He is a member of the Transformational Leadership Council.

Find out more about Barnet at www.barnetbain.com.

# Daily Cup of Calm

## by Kelle Sutliff

In my twelve years of experience helping people follow their intuition, alleviate stress, and lead productive and peaceful lives, I've found that one of the most valuable things you can do is to start your day by grounding yourself physically, mentally, and spiritually. Doing so will allow you to focus your inner energy in the right direction and bring you peace and serenity throughout your day, regardless of the circumstances going on around you.

I regularly tell my clients that the most important gift you can give to yourself is to connect with the physical and spiritual aspects of yourself, and by combining those two together into a daily practice, you have the recipe for calm.

I know, easier said than done. Well, please listen as I outline a morning plan for doing just that, and you'll be surprised to learn that it takes about as much time as making your morning cup of java.

When you wake up in the morning, find a quiet spot in your home where you can be undisturbed for three minutes. Maybe you have a garden outside, a sitting room in your home, or—if privacy is hard to come by—you can always lock yourself in the bathroom!

Once you have found your place of refuge, claim it as your sacred spot for the next few minutes. Take a few deep breaths. Close your eyes and begin to envision a white light showering down on you. As this white light hits the crown of your head, surrender your worries and state your intentions for your day. Say things like, "I am calm with my children," "I am closing that business deal today," "I am healed from cancer." These affirmations will be different for each of us, so remember to be very focused on and specific about whatever your particular prayer or intention is. Make sure you say it in the present tense. By doing so, you give the universe the green light to make it happen today, not ten years from now. For example, don't say, "I hope this is going to happen." Hope can give the universe the yellow light, the pause to yield to a later time. You want your energy and intention to work instantly. So remember to always state your intentions in present tense while you envision them happening *now*.

As you keep pulling this light down through your body, picture it passing through your forehead, throat, heart, stomach, knees, and feet. All these body parts have energy points called chakras. These chakras hold energy. If any are out of alignment, it is usually those places in the physical body where we get sick. By envisioning the healing light descending on your body and stating your intentions for the day, you are clearing your system, purifying your energy field, and dissolving any pent-up negativity.

As the white light showers over and through you, envision your feet anchoring you to the earth, grounding you strongly in the power of your own self. Like a tall and powerful tree, you are now planted for the day ahead, drawing on the protective white light the way a tree draws energy from the sun.

Open your eyes.

That's it! See I told you this exercise was quick. With daily practice, this simple, powerful exercise will connect your physical body and your spiritual self, creating balance, harmony, and peace throughout your day, all in the same amount of time it takes to make your morning cup of coffee.

KELLE SUTLIFF is a psychic medium and writer living in Andover, Massachusetts.

Visit her website at www.psychicmediumreads.com.

# Creativity:
# The Recipe for Awakening

## by Renee Baribeau

While speaking about the benefits of his meditative practice, Ram Dass noted a grandmotherly woman in the front row who nodded her smiling agreement with each statement he made. Curious as to what tradition she followed, he made a point to approach her afterward and ask about her own practice. She leaned forward and whispered in a confidential voice: "I knit."

To the chef/woman I was twenty five years ago, the idea that knitting, painting, or even cooking could be a legitimate path to spiritual development was alien to me. As far as I was concerned, meditation was a sport for sissies. Life was to be lived. It was juicy meat sliced with an electric knife for easy consumption. And besides, commanding a kitchen staff for fourteen hours a day left no time for quiet contemplation. Desperation, though, has a funny way of forcing a shift in a good cook's recipe.

I threw my requisite shovel of dirt onto my father's casket and headed out immediately after his funeral. I drove four hours to meet with a client who smiled a phony smile and said, "Sorry about your father." Then, without taking a breath, he continued, "Now! On to my daughter's wedding."

My silence implied yes, but my rage imploded no, devouring me in a seething burn. I mark that moment as the beginning of my descent into a creative black hole. A few days later found me grief-stricken and crumpled on the terracotta tile floor of my restaurant kitchen, screaming at God that I could not stand to cook for one more wedding, anniversary, birthday, retirement, or any other special occasion.

Yet cooking was what I did and who I was. I was yoked to my work, though my stock pot was scorched dry and crusted black. When the bride celebrated her second anniversary by filing for divorce and throwing a party, I found myself on my knees once again, begging for one more artful idea to see me through yet another "occasion." The idea that showed up this time was a doozy. It was the last original idea I was to have for some time. Burnout set up in me like custard in a mold. Faced with a deepening depression and exhaustion, my therapist declared "rest."

Behind the locked doors of a mental ward, my anger exposed its raw, pungent self, like a clove of garlic pressed too hard, when they dared to place me on a food disorder unit; there were no beds for heartbreak. I threw a grand tantrum and let them know that I, Renee Danielle Baribeau, was a *chef!* How could I possibly observe Rule #1, which was "Do not talk about food"? Food was my show plate and the trophy that depicted my value!

Just imagine that you are the blue and orange fire on the tip of a match. Now blow out the flame and look at what's left. That is exactly how I felt when they cut me off from what I insisted was my very life's breath. Sipping my Coca-Cola and feeling like a queen in my resolute huff—the only passenger aboard my private jet—I had no idea that I was beginning what would be a twenty-year solo quest for awakening. I could not have believed it then.

The best I can say about this period of enforced abstinence from my former passion was that it gave me the clarity I needed to see that my self-worth had been a poorly seasoned dish from the beginning. Diagnosed with burnout and sent home after ten days, I was still unable to bring myself to return to the kitchen. It would be quite a while before I did.

Art therapy was to become an integral component of my treatment. At first, it only revealed what I had ignored for a very long time, memories like rotting fruit tucked away in the frosted glass drawers of my emotional refrigerator.

But then, while sitting on the stoop one day admiring the brightly colored tulips and leafing through a children's watercolor book,[1] my phone rang. The caller was my mother, who immediately said, "You're painting?! You were never creative!"

Another layer of the onion that was *me* peeled back as I recalled that I had first gotten that message way back at the age of six, when Mom had dismissed my painting of a half-eaten hotdog—my interpreta-

tion of *The Last Supper,* which was done as an assign-
ment in Bible class. I had been so proud of my work
and so shocked, surprised, and puzzled by her reaction. Wow. Mom, food, creativity, need for approval.
Maybe they were all connected.

I continued to paint in spite of her negative
proclamation. At first, my efforts were only squiggly
water marks on paper. As I recovered, I moved on
to drawing stick figures, and finally to painting on
canvas. Today, colorful paintings fill the walls of my
home, and I think of them as the maps of my healing journey.

Creative burnout was both the salty finish and the
first ingredient toward my spiritual awakening. My
ability to cook was being restored in the process, but
it would still take years before I was as fluent in the
kitchen as I had once been. That came only after I discovered the silence that was present when I painted.
Then I remembered how it felt to be the most critical
ingredient in the alchemical process, and later on, as
I began to cook again, I felt that I had come home to
myself once again.

In that silence lived the endless and eternal magi-
cal mixing of colors and flavors that was unpredictable

and constant. Today I work as a healer, and I cook for fun. To be confronted by a cutting board, a knife, and fresh vegetables is like facing a blank canvas with a boxful of colorful acrylics.

Any activity you love can be a contemplative practice leading to your own spiritual growth, but to engage fully in life, we must allow it to flow through us. Now, when I hear my own clients say, "I am not creative," I wonder what adult convinced them of that at a young age. Then I take out my finger paints so that they can explore themselves.

Creativity is akin to spirituality and is the yard-stick I use to measure joy. There are many recipes for enlightenment. Washing the car or dicing an onion works equally as well as humming a chant, *if* one is purposefully present. We are all given creative gifts freely at birth; they can be taken away by neglect, overwork, judgmental adults, or heartbreak. In my experience of working with clients, I have witnessed that apathy, depression, heartbreak, and the lack of creative expression or compliments may be the root causes of psychosis, ADD, and other disorders. A clever balance is the key to utilizing a hobby as a form of meditation.

Due to chronic heartbreak, I lost my passion, and it was necessary to find it again. So, now, like the woman who knits, I cook. Friends tell me I cook like a painter, and they could pay me no finer compliment.

﹡

RENEE BARIBEAU, the Practical Shaman, transforms everyday experience into tales of healing and human renovation. This story is an excerpt from *The Shaman Chef, My Life and Other Recipes*, which will be released in spring 2012. As a chef, she lives in the domain of food as the metaphor for life.

Visit her website at www.ThePracticalShaman.com.

# Pardon Me:
# Finding Authentic Forgiveness

## by Chantal Herman

So there I was, sitting with my friend Rose, listening to yet another incident in which her boss had disrespected her at work. She told me how this "bully of the boardroom" hardly acknowledged anyone's existence and wouldn't admit to any weakness of her own. As I listened to Rose, my first instinct was to agree with her viewpoint and be the sympathetic ear she wanted. But this day, I held back. The scenario was all too familiar, and I wanted a different outcome for Rose.

I had been in similar tyrant/victim situations, and I, like my friend, was sick of feeling angry and powerless. As she spoke, I became aware of how Rose—even though talking about a past event—was still experiencing her victimhood very much in the present without her boss even needing to be there!

What an amazing realization. Here my friend Rose was, hurting and blaming her pain on some-one else, someone who wasn't even in the room. It occurred to me that there was only one person who could be hurting Rose at this moment, and it was her-self! As soon as she accepted her boss's criticism as fact, she became the bully herself. She locked herself into her victim identity where she no longer needed an outside perpetrator. Instead, she bullied herself into feeling powerless. As I looked at my own life, I saw how oftentimes I, too, had been my own worst critic. I realized that it is one of the worst and most common traits that we share as human beings.

Just think for a moment to the last time you tried something, and it didn't work out as you had planned. How did you treat yourself in your moment of vulner-ability and guilt? Did you take yourself by the hand and say, "Hey, it's all right. It didn't work today, but tomorrow we'll create something more amazing"? If you did, well done! But I'm willing to bet the conversation went more like this: "You messed up again! I don't know why you even bother. Just give up now and save yourself the embarrassment of people seeing you for what you are—worthless."

Yes, we are our own biggest bullies. It's the one thing that we don't want to admit because it is shameful; instead, we find someone outside ourselves to take responsibility for causing our pain. But no matter how much you feel you need the outside perpetrator's apology, kindness, or admission of guilt, it will never satisfy you, because the true damage and disrespect was committed by you first and, thus, can only be healed by you.

You can begin to heal yourself by acknowledging that no one is served by your abuse of yourself. You are your own victim, you are keeping yourself small and limited. You have accepted the abuse. So now apologize to yourself for the damage you have done to yourself, and forgive yourself for not being supportive when you needed it the most. Forgive yourself for allowing yourself to become a victim.

If you can, you will have broken the chain that you created and free yourself, your supposed tyrant, and anyone else whom you may have blamed for how you felt about yourself. It is time to take yourself gently by the hand and refuse to buy into the error that anything outside us has the capacity to give us something that we already possess: wholeness.

Life is ever-changing wholeness, flow, expansiveness, joy, and possibility in creation. As part of creation, it stands to reason that I, too, am naturally drawn to experience and live that flow, limitlessness, and joy, because I am part of it. The only thing standing in the way of experiencing that freedom is the other part of myself, born in separateness and with the need to label and judge things, solidify them— make them (and my identity) *real*—to feel secure. Authentic forgiveness is letting go of our labels, our tyrant/victim mentalities. It is self-forgiveness and an invitation to step into the boundless joy of Life. It is part of the free-flowing aspect of the self and a choice that every person has the ability to make.

Everything *wants* to move, to become. It is part of Life—of natural evolution. It makes sense that for us to evolve and experience freedom, we need to overcome our "stuckness," our solidified identity. We do that by dropping the labels and letting go of our need to keep them.

In wholeness, there is no truth in the Tyrant, and there is no truth in the Victim. Neither label exists except in our finite, separate self. We are everything and nothing, boundless yet insignificant, cause and effect, separate yet connected—all at the same time. And it is only when we forgive ourselves that we will see that *there was no tyrant in the first place,* only a messenger alerting us to the presence of a hardened aspect of our identity that has *wanted* to shift all along.

It is worth noting that the Sanskrit word for the heart chakra, Anahata, means "unstuck."

So the next time Rose feels that her tyrannical boss is belittling her work, she will stop to think, "Who is really the bully here?" Once she acknowledges how she has been abusing herself, she can forgive herself and her boss and choose to move from a space of victimization into true, authentic forgiveness. I hope you will do the same.

CHANTAL HERMAN is the author of *It Is All about You: Know Your Power, Drop Your Obstacles, and Step into the Life You Want—Now.* She is a Messenger of Change with the Movement of Change and, as a Transformation Catalyst and Coach, she has developed the Involutions Process that helps people release through giving themselves what they crave most from the outside world.

See her website at www.chantalherman.com.

# Trust Your Body's Intuition

## by Asia Voight

You *never* expect it to happen to you.

My heart vibrated in terror. My legs wouldn't move. Would I be paralyzed forever? My lungs felt like someone had poured cement into them. I could barely take a breath. I lay in a North Florida burn unit wedded to my hospital bed after a fiery car accident.

"She has a 3 percent chance of survival." The words of the doctor bounced off the ER walls as my mother collapsed. "She's young. If she makes it, she'll be 98 percent disabled."

Two months later, miraculously having survived torturous daily burn care, a respirator, and eleven surgeries, my legs remained immobile. The new development of a skin graft–induced "drop foot," which hung at the end of my numb leg, sealed the fact that I might never walk. Hunched like a ward of the state among crisp white sheets, I cried.

Flinging open the dingy yellow curtain, my nurse informed me that a neurologist was on his way. The fluorescent lights humming above me seemed to dim, as if the black smoke from my car accident had returned. *Something needs to change,* I thought weakly. Suddenly, a sweet reminder of my intuitive connection with animals, spirit guides, and angels rushed through me. These incredible beings gave me peace. I needed their help more than ever.

*Call on them again.* This idea came to me from deep inside these memories. I desired to feel their presence and hear their wise guidance.

*Angels, animals, and spirit guides, please help me!* I begged silently to those who might be listening.

Startled by a repetitive clang, I opened my eyes. The lanky, white-coated neurologist marched into the room pushing an imposing computer cart. Operating a multifarious machine, he scanned, poked, and prodded my legs, occasionally taking a hiatus to inquisitively squint up at me.

After analyzing the data, he stated, "There's no response whatsoever in your left leg. It's paralyzed. *It is unlikely you will ever walk again.*" His sterile voice hung there.

Bam! My stomach turned inside-out. No one wants to hear those words, but this hit was different. My body intelligence blasted a "That's not my truth" response. *Could this be so?* Scared of being wrong, I waited for a confirming sensation from my spiritual friends. Nothing. Panicked, I asked again. "Please send me a message. Will I walk? My body is saying he's not right!"

Relief came through the gentle pressure of my spirit guide's hand on my back. He spoke to me in a whisper, "Come here, lean and let go into my touch." I did. I leaned into him. My breathing slowed, and the space between each breath became longer. In between the breaths, a distinctive kind of space emerged—a *pause.* This pause became a portal to a greater spaciousness within and without. I found myself in the gap between breaths, the pause between words.

"I've felt this expanded feeling before," I said to my guide.

"Yes," he responded.

"I'm not sure what this is about, though."

"This is the *pause*. The *pause* is where you will begin to find the answer concerning your legs. Your body knows how to listen and move with energy and create this opening that leads to direct access to Universal wisdom. This opening is the *pause*."

Then a scene from my past unfolded:

> I recognized the red brick apartments next to my childhood home. Two older girls called me over to an empty parking lot where they were playing jump rope. Each held the smooth wooden handle of the thick rope as they swung it overhead in unison.
>
> "Jump in," the brown-haired girl squealed. The dirty-white rope thumped on the worn blacktop.
>
> "I don't know how," I shyly called back.
>
> "Put your hands in the air and follow the movement of the rope. When you see an opening, hop in."
>
> I did what she said, but repeatedly the rope slapped me in the back or hit me in the face. "I can't do it," I said, as I shrank.

Undaunted, the girls kept the rope moving through the air. "You're trying too hard and rushing. Start again and this time shut your eyes and *feel* the opening."

Lifting my arms up to shoulder height, I imitated the rope's movement. Then I closed my eyes; my inner eye opened, and the rope became a streaming, dark-purple arch. The open space became an obvious energetic *pause.*

I felt illuminated from within as I confidently stepped into the center. My feet jumped in rhythm as the girls started singing and alternately jumping in place while keeping us all in perfect synchronicity like African Maasai dancers. The energy space around us began to expand and pulse as if we were floating above the earth.

Opening my eyes in my hospital bed, I felt the hand of my guide. "That's the feeling and rhythm you can use now to lead to the *pause* and to go into the expanded space of the Divine. Your answer waits for you there."

Imagining the jump-rope rhythm, I closed my eyes and felt my breath at the same time. The edges of the "rope" began to get larger. I stepped into the open space. When I reached the center, the rhythm stopped, and I stood in the quiet of the *pause.* As I exhaled within the *pause,* a platform appeared suspended in a dark yet starlit space. I stepped onto the platform; the length expanded, allowing me to walk into the core of the universe. I heard divinity simply say, "You will walk."

A second later I was back in the room, and my spirit guide sent a soft cool breeze onto my charred, raw leg—the very one the neurologist had said I had no feeling in. The doubt and fear of not walking suddenly dropped away like boulders tumbling down a mountainside.

Now peacefully cognizant that the neurologist's prognosis did not resonate with my body, I calmly asked him to leave. He didn't.

"You have to accept the facts," he said, looming toward my face.

Instead of being scared, my intuitive connection made me feel potent with passion, and I proclaimed aloud, "I will walk!"

Hearing the commotion, my regular doctor, with his grandfatherly manner, came walking up to my bedside, waving his arms and shooing the babbling neurologist toward the ICU's swinging doors.

"I've seen people heal this," he said, rubbing his

chin and looking at my leg. His encouragement gave me the final boost.

"People heal, and so will I," became my daily mantra to my leg. I said it with love and confidence.

Clearly, my body agreed; it regenerated my nerves, and, in only three weeks, I walked!

Next time you need healing guidance, ask your spirit guides, animal helpers, or angels to assist you; listen to your body, trust, feel the rhythm, and step into the *pause of the divine*. There universal wisdom quietly abides, ready to give you the answers you seek.

ASIA VOIGHT is an internationally known intuitive guide, animal communicator, teacher, and author. Her work has been featured on ABC, NBC, and Fox TV, as well as in countless radio interviews. She has been featured in many publications such as *Brava* and *Women* magazines, the *Wisconsin State Journal*, and the *Fitchburg Star*.

In her animal communication and intuitive development workshops, Asia shares her skills by gently guiding course participants to connect with their own intuition through a variety of exercises and guided meditations.

Watch for Asia's upcoming book, *Burned Back to Spirit: Awakening Your Intuitive Powers by Way of One Woman's Near-Death Experience.*

Visit her website at www.AsiaVoight.com.

# The Five-Second Secret to Relaxation

by Wendy Beyer

To be honest, I don't know how on earth this woman ever ended up making the phone call to schedule an appointment with me, a colon hydrotherapist, let alone land here on my table at this precise and defining moment of all colonic sessions wherein I'm inserting the speculum into her rectum for the first time. She's so nervous, she is a battened-down fortress. Practically impenetrable unless I can outwit her stalwart team of reflexes and breach security. No small task when dealing with the high-strung, highly successful, pumped-up professionals of the world. Getting someone of this ilk to relax in this situation is akin to cracking the Da Vinci Code. The Holy Grail lies within.

How, then, am I going to help this woman relax?

Of course there's more going on with Dorothy on the stress continuum than her tough exterior posterior. She's got a mother with Alzheimer's whom she adores, but Dorothy has recently been solely responsible for placing her in an assisted-care facility. Dorothy visits daily, on top of working sixty-plus hours a week. She's got a high-profile corporate job where she's kicking serious butt and a boss who resents her for it, thus embroiling her in a sticky human resources wrangle. Plus, she's got a history of poverty and addiction; although she triumphed over it decades ago, its undercurrent of fear and vigilance is still a continuous babbling brook trickling through her psyche. The woman has her reasons for being clenched.

Her body has pushed her to an edge of discomfort that she never imagined she'd be in, given all her self-discipline and achievement and security. Her tummy has been in an uproar for weeks, and the doctors just keep telling her to drink more water and eat more fiber, neither of which is helping.

"Well, Dorothy," I say, "am I going to have to buy you dinner and drinks first or what?"

Thankfully she chuckles. Which gets her breathing. This may sound cliché, but all the experts will agree that this will go a long way toward putting her in a state of relaxation.

Then I invite her to remember why she's here, reminding her that she's the smart, loving one who took off work at a decent hour to come here and give herself some healing. "Seriously, Dorothy, have a simple private conversation in your mind right now, and let it know that it's okay to relax and have this procedure. Remind it why you're doing this."

And I'll be doggoned if her colon doesn't relax right there on the spot and that speculum doesn't just slip right in!

What I love is how delighted Dorothy is with her ability to relax her own body, and how quickly her mood and energy have shifted. Her whole demeanor relaxes as she laughs and says, "Wow! I had no idea I was *that* uptight!"

"Right? Who knew!?" I chime in. "And how 'bout the part where it took you all of about five seconds of focused intention to turn this whole situation around?"

"Unbelievable."

"You don't have to wait until the next time your colon is in a sketchy situation to utilize this principle, you know."

Another hearty laugh from Dorothy ushers us into the real work that we accomplish during her visits with me. Mainly, she learns to relax. During our weeks of work together, she explores the truth that it doesn't take a weekend retreat, an impeccable meditation practice, or a secret handshake to access the mind/body/spirit connection.

How did Dorothy learn to relax? Any time she noticed that she was stressed out, she simply remembered how quickly and easily her body responded when she tuned in to it during that first colonic session. She figured that if she could help her body calm down that quickly, and in that heightened situation, she could do it anywhere, anytime. And she's right. As Dorothy discovered on the table that day, the answer lies within. Stop, take a breath, tune in to your body. It will tell you what you need.

What your body tells you may sometimes surprise you. Instead of getting more serious about relaxation, you may discover that you need to watch a funny movie to get yourself laughing or dance in your living room to your favorite song from the '80s when no one is watching. Or you may find that all you needed was the pure, simple act of bringing your attention back to *you* and voila, stress diminishes. Do whatever it is that shifts your perspective and vibration, even if only for a few minutes. It gets easier and easier to choose it the more you tune in and do it. From there, start reaping the benefits.

Dorothy is sleeping better, she tells me. As her colon hydrotherapist, I can attest to how easy her sessions are now. I only see her occasionally for maintenance sessions, which are filled with wonderful updates.

All her fun relaxation experiments have freed up her psyche to start really looking at what she may be holding on to in her life: her routines, her attitudes, and any other unconscious aspects that are no longer relevant, no longer serving her. From that exploration, she is exercising differently, spending more time with friends, and actually using her vacation time, instead of rolling it over. Time out for relaxation begets more time for relaxation!

She even got a promotion at work. True story!

She still visits her mom daily, but it's easier now, she says; she's less stressed. She says she has a neutrality now and a sense of trust and flow that she never used to have.

All as the result of simply learning how to relax!

WENDY BEYER is a colon hydrotherapist and has served clients professionally for twenty years. Her personal mission is to remove the fear and taboo attached to caring for one's colon. She shares a wealth of information about detoxification and cleansing with her clients, but she has discovered that most challenges to digestion, assimilation, and elimination resolve quickly by simply teaching her clients to reconnect with their "gut-feelings."

For more information, please visit
www.wendycolonhydrotherapy.com.

# Just Being You:
# The Secret to Inner Bliss

## by Siobhan Coulter

Do you glow from the inside out? I'm not talking about consuming vitamins or using the latest skin care applications. I'm talking about connecting with your inner joy and letting it glow from every pore of your body; about letting your power, your happiness, and your light shine out and illuminate the world around you.

Instinctively, we all want to access our inner bliss and live in our natural state of happiness, but unfortunately most of us have forgotten how to do this.

There are lots of ways that people *try* to feel that

inner bliss: buying new things such as toys, clothes, games, and gadgets, but if you look at those people closely, you'll see that they only glow from the outside.

Now there is nothing *wrong* with them using things to make themselves glow on the outside, but it doesn't last. These new things will gradually become old and dull, so they end up in an endless search for new things to have, to do, and to buy to make them glow from the outside. Of course, whether they know it or not, what they really want is to find their inner bliss that can make them glow on the inside.

Glowing from the inside out is *not* about things, it is about **Being.** Not *being* perfect, wonderful, fashionable, or rich. About **Being You.** You don't have to buy anything! Just **Be You.**

**Being You** means doing things that *you* like to do. Not because they will make you perfect, wonderful, fashionable, or rich. Do things, make things, buy things that *you* want to do, make, or buy. Things that touch the very core of who you are. Things that make your heart sing, that are fun, that bring you joy and make you laugh.

When you are feeling your inner bliss, you'll want to feel more of it, all of the time, so you will naturally begin to gravitate toward activities that bring out your bliss. Your only task here is to let it happen and just go with the flow.

Remember, doing something that brings you in touch with your inner bliss isn't automatically going to make you the World's Number One at that activity. You might not be good at it at all. But it's not about being perfect or even doing it perfectly, it is about *enjoying yourself* while you are doing it. Who cares if you never actually knit a jumper or become a master at painting. What matters is that you love the click-clack of knitting needles or that your heart soars when you put brush to canvas.

When you start a new activity that requires some skill to master it, please give yourself enough time, space, and practice to gain those skills *before* you put it in the "No Bliss Basket." After all, when you finally connect that racket with the ball, you might actually really enjoy tennis!

Here is a little creative visualization exercise to give you a taste of what following your inner bliss feels like:

Imagine yourself doing something you love to do. Really go for it. Imagine how good it feels and how happy you are. Now feel your bliss growing inside you.

Now let your bliss grow and come up and out. Imagine it's like the most amazing starlight shining out from the very core of you and from every pore of your body. Pause and allow yourself to sit in that feeling.

Wow! You look great! And by the way, you are now glowing from the inside out!

When you are glowing from the inside out, you are standing in your power and connecting with your soul's joy—your inner bliss—and that, my friend, is what life is all about. You feel complete, joyous, and free. It is glorious, it is achievable, and it is so easy to do. Go for it!

SIOBHAN COULTER is a psychologist and energy worker specializing in past-life regression therapy. Siobhan's passion for her own life-healing journey led her to undertake extensive post-graduate study into personal empowerment and to open her own private practice in Australia. She is passionate about supporting others to embrace their own empowered energy, so they can create a life that is complete, joyous, and free. Siobhan currently lives in Singapore with her loving husband and beautiful twin boys. This is her first published work.

# Awful Gifts:
# Blessings in Disguise

## by Sheila Pearl, MSW

Sometimes our worst nightmares happen. We find ourselves asking questions like, "Why me?" We wonder how we are going to survive the seemingly awful circumstances that appear in our lives. Sometimes, we may even wonder if we *want* to survive the nightmare at all.

But synchronicity is happening around us all the time; those seemingly random coincidences are trying to tell us something. Our problems and painful circumstances are really opportunities that serve to help us evolve in our awareness and consciousness.

As much as my husband's dementia was our worst nightmare, I have grown to see that awful time in our lives as an awesome gift.

One day, my husband, Aaron, saw a bright flash and fell backwards, as if someone had pushed him. After that episode, there were more spontaneous flashes and then falling. He started to have problems, such as getting lost going to a cemetery for a funeral or arriving late to appointments. Aaron was never late! He would lose focus while giving a sermon. His falling and disturbed orientation became common. Aaron had witnessed his grandmother's dementia, and he lived with a lifelong fear of experiencing what she had gone through.

Aaron did not believe in an afterlife. Although he embraced mainstream Judaism, Aaron rejected Jewish mysticism, Kabbalah. Aaron was a rational intellectual: he had a scientific mindset and mocked the validity of intuition. He didn't like my suggestion that he was intuitive, although when he first saw me, he announced to friends, "I'm going to marry that woman!"

Aaron prized his mind above all else. He would exclaim, "When I don't know who you are, shoot me!" However, whenever I asked him if he was ready to die, he protested, "No! . . . I'm afraid to die!" Fear became our constant companion.

For five years Aaron was stuck in his bed, out of his mind. I screamed, "How much longer?" I felt outrage at the injustice, that this cruel disease could rob a brilliant orator and teacher of his dignity and strip me of my serenity. Our savings and retirement funds were wiped out, and our beautiful home was in foreclosure. I was feeling afraid, trapped, angry, and helpless.

I became an escape artist: I kept very busy working, and that allowed me to stay away from home and avoid facing Aaron and the illness. Worried about my emotional state, friends in Israel invited me for respite. There, I met Yoram, who told me he was "sent" to me with a message: "Go home and give your husband unconditional love; stay close to him and receive the gift of this journey. Receive the gift. . . ."

This seemed an unlikely solution, but in desperation, I was willing to try anything.

When I returned home, I evaluated the gifts and tools I had been gathering in Israel while I was away. I had been learning how to communicate spirit to spirit, a technique for "tuning in" called "kything," a process by which two people can wordlessly communicate by using their intuition. I was learning how to tune in to my intuitive wisdom. I became more aware of the synchronicity all around, in the teachers who were showing up and in the people, like Yoram, who brought me messages.

One day, as I was meditating in Aaron's room, I heard his voice in my intuitive mind: "I am not my body. I am not my mind. I am not my brain. Now I know that. Everything is energy . . . and energy doesn't die. When my body dies, there is still life." I felt a rush of adrenaline throughout my body. What was I hearing? Was that *really* Aaron communicating with me, spirit to spirit? I was startled and incredulous, but decided to continue to listen. He added, "Keep listening . . . finally you found the pathway to hear my voice. Just keep listening. . . ."

I broke out in a cold sweat. I realized that it was highly likely I was "just imagining things." Imagination, in its essence, is the opportunity to allow another realm of reality into my heart and mind, and I realized that what I might be "imagining" could as easily be a real communication from Aaron as my own wishful thinking.

In any event, I was getting some messages. I

decided to keep listening. I continued to kythe with him. My kything became a regular practice with Aaron, my friends, and my clients. One synchronicity after another continued to occur, multiplying, as I remained open to listening.

As my intuitive communications with Aaron increased, he became more awake and alert. When he became more lucid for extended periods of time, we even had voice-to-voice conversations, in addition to our intuitive exchanges. His nurses were shocked by the transformation in his energy and alertness. Yes, he would still drift off to other distant planets and dimensions, and I often wondered where he was. But in our stillness, he would communicate about jumping into other dimensions of consciousness. Where once there was fear, now there was wonder. Where once there was anger and rage, there was now surrender and serenity.

One day, shortly before his death, he intuitively told me that he no longer feared death. He described a "knowing" that there is no death. He told me he couldn't imagine leaving me; his body would die, but *he* would always be with me.

On April 1, 2005, Aaron's nurse called me: "He

refuses to eat! What should I do?" I knew . . . Aaron was ready. (That day, the pope also died; I actually imagined that he invited Aaron to join him!) When I reached Aaron's bedside, I noticed that he was alert, almost defiant, and had clear eyes, not foggy.

I asked, "Are you ready to go, my darling?"

He stared at me knowingly, "Yes . . . I am."

I asked, "Not afraid of death?"

He answered resolutely, "No, I'm ready."

I instructed the nurse to stop offering food or fluids; explaining he was ready to let go. The releasing process took one week. On his "Continuation Day," I held his hand and kept my breathing synchronized to his as he neared his final release. While he had still been alert earlier in the day, I asked for a kiss, which he gave me as he whispered, "Goodbye, sweetness . . ." That evening, with his last breath, I felt as if we were giving birth!

For me, that awful illness became one of my most awesome gifts and blessings. I shared the very substance of life with my husband. During that process, I learned that life is more than we could possibly imagine: that we are not our bodies or our brains and that the illness of dementia is an opportunity to witness the transition process in slow motion, to experience the many dimensions of consciousness available to human beings when we allow for stillness and simply listen.

So the next time an "awful gift" comes your way, I hope you can find the awesome blessing underneath it.

SHEILA PEARL, MSW, is a life coach and speaks at many events in the New York area. She was a finalist in the 2011 "Next Top Self-Help Author" contest, and her previous book, *Ageless & Sexy*, was published in Fall 2011. Her next book, *Looking for the Gift: Conscious Conversations on Facing Adversity*, which has a foreword by Neale Donald Walsch, is scheduled to be released in 2012. She is also the author of *Still Life: A Spiritual Guidebook for Life Transitions; Wake Up Women: Be Happy, Healthy, & Wealthy;* and coauthor of *The Winning Connection.*

# You're Already Enough

## by Susan Barker

*Judgment and love are opposites. From one
come all the sorrows of the world. But from the other
comes the peace of God.*

—A Course in Miracles

We didn't arrive in this world as beautiful babies
disapproving of ourselves or others. It was a learned
behavior, a learned response to conditional love
based on approval and disapproval. Even those of
us who felt very loved as children encountered situations in which we learned that love and acceptance

was conditional on how we acted, how we looked, and on what we achieved. But the Truth is, you were born worthy simply because you are. Nothing you do or don't do in this life changes that. A Course in Miracles says: "Your worth is not established by teaching or learning. Your worth is established by God. Nothing you do or think or wish or make is necessary to establish your worth."

Take that in for a moment; sit with it, feel it, breathe it in. Reading that passage and feeling the truth of it was a real awakening for me. Prior to this realization, my whole life had been spent trying to be worthy. That has meant different things at different times. It has meant trying to be thin, pretty, and an A student. It meant being witty, earning degrees, being liked, saying yes" when I meant "no," having a boyfriend, husband, children. It has meant having and keeping a job, paying my bills, owning a house, being an upstanding citizen, etc., etc. All of these have to do with gaining the approval of family and society. None of them have to do with real self-worth.

We can all feel the truth of our worth in our hearts and souls, though we may not realize it at first. Yet the Truth that you and I and everyone else were born worthy of unconditional love is a foreign or forgotten idea to many of us. We say we love ourselves, but our mind is full of self-talk like this: I wish I didn't have this tummy bulge. I wish my hair was thicker, my nose was smaller, and I wasn't aging. I wish I didn't have this mole on my neck, that I was smarter, made more money, had a man, had a woman, that my father approved of me, or that my mom understood me. The list goes on ad infinitum.

It's hard to feel worthy and full of unconditional love when we are judging ourselves so harshly. For most of us, the worst tyrant in our lives is the one that lives in our head. Think about it, you would never say to someone else the denigrating things that you say to yourself. But if you listen to the self-talk in your head, you'll find that you spend so much of your time judging yourself that it makes self-love impossible.

Some people say that if we stop judging ourselves, we won't be able to keep moving forward and accomplishing our goals. But just because this has been taught for generation after generation, doesn't make it true. Fear, judgment, and competition have shaped our society and our well-being. These motivational "tools" don't work because we aren't happy with our own levels of joy, peace, and satisfaction.

Let's turn it around. You are worthy simply because you are. That means you can trust yourself to thrive in love. That means you can trust us all to thrive in love. What would be different in your life if you began with the knowledge that you are worthy of heaven right here on earth and so is everyone else? Imagine it. Perhaps you would stop pouring all your energy into trying to *be* enough and realize that you already *are* enough. If you were to experience the joy, love, and peace that is your birthright, you would traverse the ups and downs of your life journey with a confidence born of inherent self-worth. You would no longer need to compete for prestige or resources, because if we are all worthy beings, then we would live in a respectful and abundant world. As Anais Nin wrote: "We don't see things as they are, we see things as we are."

If we are worthy because we are, then we can see, and therefore co-create through our thoughts and actions, a world that reflects just that. It is a choice to believe in the Truth that we are worthy by the Grace of our birth, and with every choice we are empowered. I invite you to love yourself, simply because you are.

SUSAN LORAINE BARKER is passionate about empowering people to love, honor, and cherish who they are. She runs experiential group play-shops in her private studio and at conferences, and she offers private Mandala, Sacred Contracts, Love Yourself, Love Your Body, and Life Empowering coaching to clients all over the world.

Susan is a graduate of Drake University and the University of Iowa and is a certified life coach and graduate of the Institute for Professional Excellence in Coaching.

Susan lives in the northwest Chicago suburbs with her husband, son, and a throng of furry and feathered friends.

To learn more about Susan's play-shops and private coaching, please visit www.themandalacoach.com.

# The Power of Conscious Choice

## by Glenyce Hughes

The moment I realized that I was creating my life through the choices I was making, I understood the power I had over my life.

Five years ago, I was deep into debt with no visible way out. I understood the Law of Attraction (LoA) to a certain degree, and, as crazy as this now sounds, I was attempting to use the LoA to create a lottery win to pay off the debt. Every week when my numbers didn't come up, I would sink lower into desperation. Although I didn't recognize it at the time, I was choosing the victim role and felt that something outside myself was the only thing that could rescue me. One night while I was sitting in self-pity and despair, I begged the Universe for help. In that moment, my intuition guided me to take action in a way that I had resisted for years. It was going to require commitment and dedication to myself. It was also going to require me choosing debt repayment over the instant gratification provided by shopping.

It was in this moment that I could clearly see how all of my previous choices had led me to this massive debt. I was absolutely responsible for where I was, not only financially but in every area of my life. I no longer had the option of blaming others or circumstances.

I followed my intuition and committed to putting all the money from the workshops I was teaching toward my debt. I didn't even allow myself to take the expenses from the workshops out of the money. Every penny went toward the debt.

As I embraced the idea that everything in my life was affected by my choices, my entire world started shifting for the better. I started to recognize that small, seemingly insignificant choices were adding up to the results I was experiencing in my life.

The choices to take a ten-minute walk after a

healthy supper and to go to bed early resulted in feel-ing better and more energized than I had in years. The choice to think positively resulted in happier feelings. The choice to be honest with others resulted in more connected relationships.

It was so exhilarating to know and feel that, through my choices, I have the power within me to completely change my life.

I didn't need a lottery win to save me. I had the power to do it by making choices that supported financial freedom, and because of this, it took me less than one year to pay off my debt.

Every choice we make has a result in our life. You can change your life for the better. It just comes down to one conscious choice after another. This means taking the time to really think about the choices you have available to you and what the possible result of each of those choices would be.

I suggest taking one area of your life that isn't work-ing for you and focus on being more conscious of the choices you are making. From there, you can start to make better choices, which will result in that area of your life changing to what you would prefer it to be. Once that area has shifted, you can move on to another.

There are times in our lives when we feel over-whelmed by what we wish to change, that the problem is just too big. We mistakenly think we have to change everything about that problem at once. But all you need to do is make one different choice to get yourself moving in the right direction. Just one, no matter how small or insignificant it may seem. Then make it again the next day. Then the next. After three days of choosing differently, you will start to feel a shift from overwhelming to doable. You will know when the shift happens because you will experience a feeling of lightness and relief. From this lightness, you can make other choices that support you in this change. These baby steps will get you where you want to go, quicker than you can imagine.

Choosing to own your ability to create your life through your choices is the most empowering thing you can do. Knowing you created something also gives you the power to know you can change what is not working. You can receive inspiration from others, but you are the one who ultimately must make the choices that change a situation or keep it the same. The choice is yours.

GLENYCE HUGHES facilitates others to live their dreams by tapping into their true power and potential. She is a leader in her field of consciousness, intuition, awareness, and energy transformation.

Her infinite love, joy, and desire to live life to the fullest is felt by everyone who encounters her and her work. Through her writing, group sessions, workshops, teleclasses, and one-on-one sessions, she is inspiring thousands to shift their limiting beliefs and live their dreams.

You can find Glenyce online at www.glenyce.net.

# The Habit of Attraction

## by Robert Evans

In 2007, I was given four life-changing words. I had reached a point in my life when I could no longer hold back the calling to become the messenger I knew I was, to truly *own* my purpose and do something good in this world that I'm passionate about.

I sat down and did the "Journal Conversation," something that I now teach. While journaling, I entered into a conversation with my "higher self," and what came forth from that conversation would change thousands of lives around the world in the years that followed.

I asked myself, "What am I passionate about?" My answer, "Making a difference, inspiring, and teaching." I then asked myself, "What kind of messages am I drawn to?" Another answer came, "Creating powerful habits and the Law of Attraction."

From that conversation came these four words: the Habit of Attraction.

That was all, though—I only had the four words, nothing else. But inside me, I had certainty and, for the first time in a long time, a willingness to detach and move forward with this intriguing four-word idea.

I sent messages to my email list, a few thousand people at the time, and I invited them to a conference call to discuss this idea. I would have been happy if only fifty people had responded. Instead, more than fifteen hundred people from around the world signed up to listen to me talk about this idea, these four words; from that moment on, I was a messenger.

The Habit of Attraction (HOA) is simple, and because of this, it works. It combines habit creation with Law of Attraction principles. I knew that I could manifest more consistently *if* I could find a way to make a "connection" to my desires/goals more often and align my energies with the energy of that desire. I knew that if I could create habits that consistently made those connections, then I could manifest anything.

Today, people who learn the Habit of Attraction and actually put it into motion in their lives see wonderful results. Of course, as with anything, it takes commitment and follow through, *but* it's simple and anyone can do it.

The HOA process is driven by three foundational principles and twenty-five different tools that are designed to help energy flow and connect you to your desires/goals.

Here are the three principles.

## It's *All* in the Energy

First, I teach becoming *aware* of four energy points: thoughts, words, feelings, and actions.

We must align these four energy points with one another. To attract and allow a desire to come forth into our lives, we need to match our energetic vibration with the energy vibration of our desire.

I believe that all of our desires already exist in the energetic field but at a vibration that we are not yet aligned with. Your job is to increase your vibration until you are of "like vibration." When that happens, you'll be able to "allow" that desire into your experience. If you can become more aware of the energy you put out and the energy you take in, you'll immediately be able to better manifest.

## Keep It Simple, Be Consistent

We flow energy every day through those four energy points, and the increase in vibration depends on how consistent we are with that energy flow. Consistency requires keeping things simple, because the moment your life or focus becomes complicated or overwhelmed, your flow stops and your vibration changes.

Imagine seeing energy as a ball of light. The moment you decide to call forth a desire, a light forms in the middle of your body. You must grow that ball of light by thinking, saying, feeling, and taking actions that align with your desire. You're expanding that light through those four energy points. The more you feed it, the greater it increases in vibration.

Keeping your manifesting simple will support the flow that makes the energy grow and will bring forth your desire faster. This is where habits come into play.

## Know Your Specific Destination

I was shocked when I asked myself what I really wanted in life because I only had basic ideas of what my desires were. I wanted more money. I wanted better health. I wanted great relationships. I wanted to live with more purpose.

None of my desires were very *specific*. But I wasn't alone. Almost everyone I taught this process to was being just as "general" as I was. I then realized why my manifesting was "hit or miss." I did not know what specific energy I needed to connect to, attract, and allow into my life. Once I defined my specific desire, I could align with its specific energy vibration.

In the HOA process, we define our specific desires through writing a Desire Statement. A Desire Statement is a supercharged affirmation that not only defines your specific desire, but it becomes your most powerful energy "activator," sending multiple streams of energy toward your desire each time you read it.

By understanding and practicing these three principles, plus the twenty-five tools I describe in my forthcoming book, *Habit of Attraction,* you can make the Law of Attraction a habit and start to build a "habit of attraction" that draws the things you really want into your life.

ROBERT EVANS is the founder of the Messenger Network and creator of the Habit of Attraction manifesting process. Robert's programs teach people how to step into their message and collectively impact the world while living a life of purpose and passion.

To learn more about Robert and the HOA process, visit www.HabitofAttraction.com.

# Visualization:
# See It to Be It

## by Glenn Groves

I was fat. I had gone from overweight to fat to obese. For nearly twenty years, I seemed to have almost no control over my weight. It was almost as if something inside me was pushing me away from being slim. Losing weight was easy. I *knew* what to do to lose weight. I just didn't do it.

Fortunately, a friend of mine told me about visualization: seeing what you want to have or how you want to be. This friend told me that when you feel good about what you visualize, you naturally move toward it.

I started to visualize "slim."

However, whenever I tried to see a picture of myself as slim, I instead saw myself as fat. I was stuck. How could I visualize slim when I could only see myself as fat? There is a simple answer. Whatever we see and feel good about is what we move toward, but it does not have to be *ourselves* that we are seeing. So I chose someone that I know who is slim (and healthy and happy) and visualized him instead. I was seeing slim.

Whenever I had spare time, I would visualize this guy and see him slim with a big, genuine smile on his face. That was easy to do, since he *is* slim and always smiling! Within a few days, the bad feelings decreased, then stopped completely. It became easy to stick to healthy foods and consume fewer calories. I no longer had to fight against the push to eat junk food and stay fat. Finally, after years of fighting the weight-loss battle, I have won the war. Twenty years ago, I started on a path from overweight to fat to obese; now, at last, I am at a healthy weight. I'm in my early forties, and I weigh what I did when I was a teenager.

Once I produced good results from visualization, I investigated why it works. The psychology behind visualization is simple and powerful.

We have two "parts" to our minds: the conscious mind and the subconscious mind.

Our subconscious "hides" thoughts and emotions (good or bad) that we don't want to remember, but it also keeps us safe from danger. *How* it keeps us safe from danger makes visualization very, very powerful.

Imagine you are inside a building, and you want to leave the building. There are three corridors you can leave by. You cannot see down the first corridor at all. You can see down the second corridor, but it feels dangerous. You can see down the third corridor, and it feels comfortable. Almost everyone will choose the third corridor. This is your subconscious keeping you safe.

Our subconscious uses two "rules of thumb" to keep us safe from danger:

1. Only go where you can see the end goal.

2. If you can see several ways to go to or through something, then go the way that feels the most comfortable or safe.

This makes sense; we cannot tell what dangers lurk in the unknown. As a general rule, things that feel comfortable to us tend to be safer than those that feel uncomfortable.

When I say that our subconscious only lets us "go" somewhere, I mean physical places *and* circumstances. You could think of being fat or slim as a circumstance.

Our subconscious "talks" to us through emotions. When it wants us to change our direction, it makes us feel depressed, cranky, uncomfortable, or stressed. We don't like these feelings, so we change things. When it wants us to head in a particular direction, it makes us feel safe and at ease in it. We like feeling this way, so we do things that move us in that direction. We can set the direction that our subconscious takes us in using visualization.

Visualization allows us to create who we are by familiarizing our subconscious minds with the direction we want to take in our lives. Once the path is familiar, our subconscious will naturally motivate us down that comfortable path. Visualization changes us from the inside out, with ease and grace.

GLENN GROVES teaches "practical psychology," tools that people can use to enhance their everyday lives. He has been leading seminars in coaching in the personal development area since 1997 and is a member of Mensa Australia.

For more information, visit
www.thefutureisfreedom.com.

# Relaxed Intention:
# A Pathway to Peace

## Leslie Gunterson

Karate is a world-renowned martial art that originated in Japan and is famous for its hand-to-hand
style of combat. But unknown to many people is that
the word "karate" literally means "empty hands." This
can mean many things to different people. To most
it means that the hands hold no weapon. According
to author Terrence Webster-Doyle, karate is "the art
of empty self."[1]

One learns through karate to empty oneself of fear
through the elimination or emptying of a personal
agenda. The emptied self is loving and thus without

fear. When you have an agenda, inherent in this is a notion that the future may not provide what you think you need without your interference.

What I have come to understand is that we all have everything we need already, but we often don't realize it. For example, take a look around the room you're sitting in, and tell me what you need in this moment that you don't already have. When we understand that we have everything we need in this moment, fear is absent. When you feel each moment as it is, lack doesn't exist. We only experience lack when we imagine the future or remember the past. By being fully in the present, we begin to feel grateful for the abundant resources we have connections with.

For most of us, remembering that we already have everything we need is easier said than done. What I recommend is what I learned to do for myself, a practice I call Relaxed Intention.

The first step is to relax. When thoughts of fear and lack arise, I acknowledge them without the internal dialogue that leads to *anxiety*. The mind chatter needs to be acknowledged first, or, like a teenager, it will argue louder until it feels it is heard. When I feel an emotional twinge of fear, loss, or regret, I don't name it. I don't work it up into anxiety by carrying on an internal dialogue about it, I just honor it: "Yes, that hurt. Yes, that was difficult." I don't justify, argue, or define my feelings. I take a deep breath, acknowledge what I feel, and let it go with my exhale.

Then comes the intention. After the acknowledgment and exhale, I consciously let the thoughts of fear and lack go. I choose instead to feel loved, abundant, and supported by the world around me. I feel all the abundance of resources in the universe. I consciously connect to the air, trees, earth, and others and feel the energy abundant in everything. Everything is here to support us.

Once I have done this, I can get on with what I am doing in my life, even if I have to do this exercise many times in the same day. By relaxing, honoring, and intending, I am able to focus on the abundance of now and relieve fear and worry.

I wish you all the best, living and loving your own purpose and vision in the world. You have nothing to lose but the fear, and every good to gain. Remember there is no lack, and you are never alone. You are always connected to everything alive around you.

Therefore, you have all of the resources you need right this minute.

Fear and love cannot co-exist. Perfect love is now, here and present. It is active love, a verb not a feeling. Perfect love is brave action and does its best for everyone, always. In the space of perfect love, there is gratitude for the abundance that is available all around us. Anxiety comes from internal conversation; but peace comes from internal quiet and resolve. The challenge is quieting the internal conversation of the past or future to feel the internal quiet and abundance in the present moment.

To return to the karate metaphor, when our hands are empty, they are also open. If you watch someone in anger and fear, their hands are usually clenched into fists. Closed hands are for fighting, defending, or hoarding. Open, empty hands are for receiving, giving, and embracing. Thus the deeper meaning of karate is the empty, open hands of giving and receiving fully with no fear of scarcity or lack. There is a quiet confidence, inner peace, and connection to the abundance of now.

Can you open your hands and relax into the now?

Leslie Gunterson is a certified performance coach, specializing in life transitions for youth, students, parents, and teachers, as well as a martial arts instructor and educator. Leslie lives in the San Francisco Bay Area and has worked in community education for more than nineteen years, both in the public and private sector. She has a master's degree in special education from Brandman University.

Her life purpose is to creatively lead, teach, and inspire herself and others toward excellence and possibilities while having fun.

# Fractals:
# Seeing the Patterns
# in Our Existence

## by Kimberly Burnham, PhD

A sometimes-forgotten ingredient for experiencing our own powerful destinies is recognizing the patterns within our bodies, the very fabric of our lives. We can more easily understand the messages around us, share our gifts, and communicate our ideas to people who can savor them when we understand how our individual cells, tissues, and organs—each with its own characteristics—fit into the whole.

French mathematician Benoit Mandelbrot coined a word to describe the wide range of geometric structures or patterns found throughout nature, including in trees, coastlines, our own branching blood-vessel "tree," the layers of tissue in the small intestines, and the neural network of our brain. The term is "fractals," and it describes the richly textured similar shapes existing everywhere. A tree is an example of a fractal in that each branch resembles a smaller version of the trunk. Even the leaves have tiny, branching veins that are similar to the branching trunk. A tree is visually complex, but it is made up of one simple branching pattern.

Fractals describe the irregularly shaped objects in our natural universe—gnarled, rough-barked pine trees, dark smoldering rain clouds, the contours of the Peruvian Andes, California's coastline. These shapes are similar within themselves, what I call "self-similar," down to the smallest levels which, it turns out, are too small even to measure. But they still provide texture to our reality.

Like a tree, your brain—that intersection of mind, body, and spirit—contains self-similar branching nerves, and, due to this fractal design, you can communicate with others and perceive the world around and inside yourself. A healthy brain can process information in a way that "fits" a personal landscape shaped by attitudes, previous knowledge, and experience. Each time you encounter something new, you change the contours of your nervous system; you change "the fit." Each time you notice something different, you extend the life of your healthy brain.

A defining feature of healthy body, mind, and spirit is adaptability—the capacity to respond to unpredictable situations, puzzling feelings, or stress. The rich, complex fractal nature of our bodies and brains suggests that we are perfectly designed to comfortably and safely enjoy life and the endless number of diverse relationships in this universe.

Even the loops of the small intestines have a fractal structure, similar to the mesmerizing contours of nested Russian dolls. Inside the loops lining the intestinal walls are tiny villi, hairlike structures that increase surface area. Found on the villi are yet more, even tinier bumps that further increase the roughness of the walls; and on these bumps are . . . well, you get the picture. Complementary medicine or nutritional regimens, such as a gluten-free diet, help to optimize the fractal nature of the digestive system's surface area.

All this surface area exists to catch the abundant sensory information within our gut, the place where important decisions are made about what to absorb and what to pass along to the large intestine. It is also the place to which we refer when having a "gut feeling," an intuition, or accessing additional information with which to make decisions. Healthier, more fractal-like guts help us create intuitive "fitness centers," so that we can access the wisdom of our subconscious mind while maintaining good boundaries with ourselves and others. Our life choices influence our gut's ability to make its own choices.

Fractal patterns invite us to look within and beyond perceived limitations, to broaden our view of the options we have, and to see how we can influence the pathways of our lives and how they are all connected. As the great naturalist John Muir said, "When we try to pick out anything by itself, we find it hitched to everything else in the universe."

Similarly, the fractal nature of our bodies, from the smallest villi to the structure of our brains, provides us with a natural process by which we can find where we fit into life's greater puzzle, simply by listening to and appreciating the self-similar patterns all around us.

KIMBERLY BURNHAM, PHD, is an integrative medicine specialist who helps people experience comfortable movement, flexibility, clarity, energy, and life—despite any diagnosis of brain, nerve, or vision dysfunction. She consults with clients in West Hartford, Connecticut, as well as across the United States and in Europe, using Integrative Medicine (energy), Matrix Energetics (information), Integrative Manual Therapy (touch), and Health Coaching (words). She is the author of *The Nerve Whisperer, Regain Your Life through Brain Health,* and a Messenger Mini-Book, *Our Fractal Nature: A Journey of Self-Discovery and Connection,* which was published under the guidance of the Messengers of Change Network. She has published a number of professional journal articles and speaks at Defeat Autism Now conferences and Alzheimer's Association meetings.

# Just Sit Down:
# A Premeditation Routine

## by Liz Byrne

Just sit down!

That's right—I'm talking to you. Or, in my New York accent, "I'm tawkin' to you!" You know who you are. You've been thinking about meditating for days, perhaps weeks or months. Maybe you have never attempted to meditate, or maybe you have tried a few times without success. It could be that you have had quite a good practice but all of a sudden find yourself unable to meditate. You've read about all the terrific things meditation might do for you—how it can alleviate stress and reduce anxiety, boost your immune system, improve memory and the ability to learn. The list goes on and on.

So if you know all of this wonderful stuff, then why aren't you meditating right now? I'll guess that it's because you can't envision stopping your brain and sitting still at this particular moment.

Well here's the good news: You are not alone. I recently found myself in a very distracted state of mind for days on end. I had a lot going on and was anxious and unable to concentrate. My meditation practice, which had been quite good for a couple of years, had fallen by the wayside. I just couldn't find the time nor could I bear the thought of sitting still.

I realized that my work, my writing practice in particular, was suffering because my brain was so busy. So there I was, trying to write, very frustrated, and looking for inspiration that just wouldn't come. So then I said to myself: "Just sit down and meditate." In fact, I said the words out loud. "Just sit down!" And I did.

I sat for about twelve minutes that day. Not a long time for me, but it was all I could handle. I continued at that pace for many days until some of my life situation straightened out, and I was calmer and able to get back to my longer, more in-depth meditations.

The reason I was able to just sit down and get back into my meditation practice is because I have a routine to call upon. Not having a routine is one of the biggest obstacles to meditation. People often just don't know where to begin. Perhaps you have read books about meditating and listened to audios guiding you along, but now you have too many ideas floating around about the "right" way to do it and don't know where to begin. All of this input can be very confusing.

Well the reality is that what you do is not as important as simply getting started. You can breathe, stretch, chant; it doesn't matter as long as you choose something that feels good for you and that you like to do. What's important is that you create your own premeditation routine, then you can call upon that whenever you want to meditate. A routine is key to assisting you in meditation because it gives you a starting point. Sometimes my premeditation routine is all I can manage to do. I get through it in about seven or eight minutes, and it relaxes me enough that I can usually maintain a meditative state of mind afterward.

The key is to do what is comfortable and easy for you, so that when you finish, you are in a relaxed position both mentally and physically.

**First, have a place to meditate.** Choose a spot in your home where it is quiet, where you feel relaxed, and where you probably won't be uninterrupted.

**Second, choose some form of decoration or symbols for that space.** You might choose candles, incense, religious items, or a favorite picture. In a corner of my bedroom, I have a small table (my altar) with two candles, an incense burner, and various items that bring me peace (a picture of my daughter when she was a baby, seashells, a gift from a friend, etc.)

**Third, get comfortable.** Pick a position to sit in. Remember, you don't have to sit in full lotus position to meditate. Nor do you have to sit on the floor. Choose a comfortable chair if that works for you. Lean up against a wall if you want the support. The key is to be comfortable. I have a good mediation cushion that I sit on with my legs casually crossed on the floor in front of it.

**Fourth, choose a couple of ways to relax yourself.** You are looking to release any stress and tension in your mind and body. Perhaps a focused-breathing exercise, some physical stretches—whatever works for you. You don't need to do a lot, just pick one or two things that feel good to you.

For example, I start with stretches for my back on the floor, then sit on my cushion and do a bit of alternate nostril breathing: Cover the left nostril, breath in through the right one, hold for a bit, breath out of the left, breath in through the left, hold for a bit, breath out of the right; repeat.

**Fifth, once you are in your comfortable position, call upon someone to join you in this moment.** Depending on your religious beliefs, you might call upon God, angels, a higher power, or perhaps a spirit guide. Or you could just thank the Universe for being present. I call upon everyone! God, the universe, my angels, animal and spirit guides.

**Sixth, and last, choose a way to focus on and relax your body.** You might think your way through a relaxation exercise, starting at your feet and working up to the top of your head. I mentally "walk" through my chakras, starting with the base or root chakra and finishing up at my crown.

Now your routine is done. By this time, you should feel relaxed and calm. If not, then simply add something or change something. The goal of the pre-meditation routine is to feel relaxed and centered by the end of it. Once you are centered and relaxed, you can begin to meditate. However you choose to meditate is fine. Choose a word, mantra, or thought that feels peaceful to you.

The important thing is to just sit down. Go to your meditation place, go through your personal routine, and see how much better you feel.

Liz Byrne is a writer, lecturer, and event producer. As the founder of Vision of One, her mission is to bring awareness to the concept of *one:* any *one* person with any *one* action in any *one* moment can make a difference in their life and in the lives of others.

After spending twenty-four years in the fields of financial services and real estate, she embarked on a career change and found herself on a personal journey of discovery. She realized that there were three very simple and personal goals that she wanted to incorporate into every decision she makes: first, to completely love what she is doing every day; second, that every decision and new venture would be in service to another person or group of people; third, that her work would involve the beauty of the arts and performance.

Liz recently completed a book entitled *Once upon a Time There Was You: Remembering Your Story.* She lives in New York with her daughter.

Visit her website at www.visiononeonline.com.

# Access Your Angels

## by Tami Gulland

When was the last time you asked your Angels for advice? If it wasn't today, then you are walking away from one of the biggest keys to your success.

People struggle with success because they don't listen to their Angels and Divine Guidance.

You may think that Angels are only available in emergencies. In fact, they are available 24/7, and they delight in assisting you in every aspect of your life, including relationships, career, health, and even money. No matter what your past or your background is or whether you have a religious affiliation or not, you have Angels that are assigned specifically to you to protect, help, and guide you. Your Angels already see you as a success and *want* you to feel successful.

Angels are messengers of love who work in concert with Source energy. Divine Guidance is the communication you receive from your Spiritual Board of Directors, or your Divine Support Team and Source. This communication can come in the form of spontaneous insights, feelings, a sense of knowing, words you hear, visions you see, synchronicities, and dreams. Your Divine Support Team can be comprised of Angels, Spirit Guides (those who have walked the path as humans before), saints, masters, and Beings of Light. Divine Guidance is the collection of insights and communication from these heavenly beings.

When we don't tune in to our Angels and Divine Guidance, we often make decisions that aren't in alignment with our core values. We live other people's agendas and grow dissatisfied with the lack of connection and meaning in our own lives. In short, we live life the hard way—isolated, inside our heads, and struggling to make things work. Think of this as being like the CEO of a large corporation and trying to do everything yourself. That would be pretty exhausting! This experience may manifest as feeling overwhelmed, stuck, and anxious; you may even run the risk of burnout. This negativity takes a huge toll on our emotional, mental, and physical health and well-being. It can contribute to stress, disease, and depression. It can also create rifts in relationships with people close to you and cause problems at work. You do not have to carry the heavy burden alone!

When you tune in to and listen to your Angels and Divine Guidance, you access the most direct route to your success. You can gain insight on where to invest your time and energy, achieve clarity on the next steps to take in your relationships and work, and learn how to shore up your internal resources for confidence.

Your Angels and Divine Team have access to the wisdom of the Universe. They are able to see the infinite possibilities for your life that may be blocked to you due to limited human perception. The great news is that you have Angels and a Divine Support Team always available to you. Whenever you ask for their advice, they give it. The key is to clear the static on your airwaves to be able to receive it.

What stands in the way of communicating with

our Angels and Divine Guidance? Being in constant motion—fight-or-flight mode—will create static on the airwaves to our Angels. When we are continually reacting to the world around us, we are often scattered. We produce results that are unfocused, ungrounded, and that take much more energy—and achieve less optimal outcomes—than when we are connected and receptive to our Divine Guidance. Attachments, ego, fear, beliefs, and control will also create static and hold us back from receiving this higher guidance.

How can you tell if you are creating static on the airwaves to your Angels?

- You feel stuck and grasp for answers or make a choice despite a gut instinct telling you otherwise.

- You fester in indecision, fearful that you may make a mistake, and obsess about the different possibilities and all the ways they could potentially go awry.

When you feel yourself in one these situations, you know it's time to clear the pathway to your Divine Guidance. Instead of staying stuck, take action to open to the simplest and most graceful path to your success: enlist the help of your Angels and Divine Team.

You can start today by following these simple steps.

1.  **Stop and breathe.** Breathe in slowly through your mouth, hold your breath for a second or two, then release the out breath with a sigh. Do this breathing three to four times in a row throughout your day. This will help take you out of fight-or-flight mode and help you more easily connect with your Angels and Divine Guidance. It will also create some space for you to be receptive to your Angels' answers.

2.  **Take your awareness to the center of your chest.** Imagine you are breathing through the center of your chest and that with each breath, your heart opens. Think of a happy memory or something or someone you love. Appreciation helps you to align to the clear, pure energy of your Angels and be more receptive to their messages.

3.  **Ask for help.** From this space, ask your Angels the question you have or for the advice you seek.

4.  **Let go and receive.** Know that the answer may come immediately, but if it doesn't, don't worry. It will come later. Continue to be curious, open, and receptive. Notice insights, feelings, and synchronicities that appear in your life.

5.  **Say thank you.** Thank your Angels and Divine Team for their love, guidance, and support.

Tami Gulland helps spiritually oriented professional women access their Angels, Divine Guidance, and answers that are authentic to them to overcome feeling stuck, disconnected, overwhelmed, and exhausted. She helps people tap in to a whole support system that is available 24/7 so that they can feel clear, empowered, supported, and spiritually connected at work and in everyday life. Tami is an Angel Therapy Practitioner, certified medium, and Angel Guide for Success.

Visit her website at www.angelsforsuccess.com.

# Be Happy
# and Success Will Follow

## by Susan McMillin

The notion that we achieve success first and happiness second is an ancient misconception. Recent scientific research shows that just the opposite is true. When we practice happiness first, success follows.

I love the way that Dr. Barbara Fredrickson, director of the Positive Emotions and Psychophysiology Lab[1] describes the essence of happiness and how to practice it: "You have within you the fuel to thrive and to flourish, and to leave this world in better shape than you found it." She goes on to say that you tap into this fuel whenever you feel energized by new ideas, at one with your surroundings, playful, creative, connected, loved, or stirred by beauty. Any time you feel positive emotions, you fuel yourself for success. You are practicing happiness whenever you purposely boost your positive emotions by smiling, seeing the best in someone or something, or being grateful for what you have.

The evolutionary link between survival and emotions is well documented. The familiar fight-or-flight response kicks in when we feel negative emotions such as anger and fear. These emotions signal danger, and our bodies prepare us to deal with danger optimally. We produce adrenaline, cortisol, and other hormones that narrow our focus to survival, prepare us for physical exertion, and shut down nonessential functions such as healing or growth.

What many people don't realize, however, is that positive emotions act on the body in much the same way: by releasing hormones that change our physical response to the world. Positive emotions release endorphins, oxytocin, and other hormones that broaden our focus and optimize our bodies for healing, growth, pleasure, and close, collaborative interactions with other people. The endorphins help us feel good, maximizing pleasure and normalizing heart rates and breathing. Our focus expands to take in more of our environment, so we are more likely to see something attractive and positive.

In addition to broadening our focus, positive emotions also prepare us to work with other people. The hormone oxytocin is often called the bonding hormone because it is high in infants and mothers during breast feeding. However, this same hormone is also present in adult men and women during close interactions with other people. When oxytocin levels are high, people forge bonds that help them work cooperatively, even in difficult situations. This enabled our ancient ancestors to hunt together, build villages, farm, and create more advanced cultures.

Just as negative emotions signal danger and a potential win-lose encounter, positive emotions signal benefits and a possible win-win encounter. When our predominant emotional state is positive, our physiology broadens our focus, making it more likely that we will see things we are attracted to.

We can reinforce our moods through our thoughts as well as our hormones. Our brains take in a lot of sensory information, more than we can process all at once. When we focus our attention closely, as in stress, we see one thing in accurate detail, but we only see that one thing. When we broaden our focus, we see lots of things, but we tend to see them in less detail—like an impressionist painting. Our brains fill in the blanks with what it expects to see. If we expect to see success, we usually do. This powerful phenomenon, often called the Pygmalion effect, has been validated repeatedly. As the great American businessman Henry Ford once said, "Whether you believe you can do a thing or not, you are right."

Not only do our positive expectations impact our own perceptions, but positive emotions are more likely to spread to others. Studies of social networks show that if a friend is in a happy mood, we are 34 percent more likely to feel happy too.[2] According to the study, bad moods do not spread as fast. So, when we improve our own mood and spread it to others, we improve our environment as well. It is easier to be happy around other happy people. After all, a happy group is a more peaceful and productive group.

Case studies have validated the connection between happiness and increased success. For example, in one study, a group of doctors were able to improve their times on a diagnostic test by 25 percent after the unexpected gift of a lollipop.[3] Not only did the doctors solve problems faster with this positive emotional boost, but the happy doctors were more likely to make the correct diagnoses than their ungifted peers. College students and preschoolers who were induced into a happy state also improved their speed and creativity in solving problems. What did it take to get these results? The doctors and the college students got a small, almost insignificant, gift, such as a lollipop or a dime. The preschoolers simply took a moment to recall a time they jumped for joy or smiled a lot. In less than a minute, all three groups increased their happiness enough to do significantly better on tests. Imagine how your performance could improve if you spent the moment before the sales call, meeting, or conversation with your teen thinking about a time you jumped for joy!

The conventional wisdom is that success breeds happiness. We mistakenly believe that we must sacrifice our current happiness to achieve the success. Then we either miss the mark or end up dissatisfied after our success. Current scientific research shows that our bodies and minds have evolved to work the other way around. The happier we are, the more effective we are at everything we try. We catch happiness when we practice it frequently every day. The more we practice, the happier and more successful we become. When we pursue happiness through success, it eludes us. But when we regularly apply ourselves to being happy, and take our happiness as a serious part of our careers and overall satisfaction, success is sure to follow.

SUSAN MCMILLIN is a high-tech engineer and project manager, who turned to the study of happiness to improve productivity—and it worked. The happier she got, the more productive and successful she became.

Now she is dedicated to finding the best teachings in happiness and spreading happiness through coaching, teaching, writing, and speaking about happiness and how to be happier at work, at play, and in life. Susan is the editor of the website www.HappyLifeU.com.

# Remember, You Always Have a Choice

by Debra L. Hanes

One of the biggest realizations we can come to in our lives is that no matter how difficult a situation seems, we always have a choice in how to handle it. We can either unconsciously react to a given situation or choose a heart-centered response. The difference with a heart-centered response is that we choose to be conscious of all that we are thinking, saying, or doing at that moment and to take responsibility for our part in the situation. With reaction, we are, by definition, unconscious of our actions and often put the blame on someone or something else. How can we move from unconsciously reacting to consciously responding in a heart-centered manner?

To make the shift, you must first ask yourself: "*How* do I wish to *be* in this life? How do I wish to be in all my relationships?" To answer this, center yourself with a few deep breaths and focus on your heart. The heart-centered answer that comes will hold true for you no matter what you face. You could answer the questions with: "I wish to be at peace and calmly face whatever comes before me." This doesn't mean you won't experience emotion. It is not about denying or suppressing what you think or feel. What it does mean is that you wish to let peace and calm direct your responses to the situations that arise in your life. It also helps you to remember that you always have a choice, even when it doesn't seem like it.

In every life situation that arises, knowing we have choices is liberating *and* frightening. It means taking full responsibility for the results of any choice we make, and sometimes that choice is to do nothing—often the hardest choice to make.

If you are going to make changes in your life to improve relationships and how you handle difficult situations, you have to make a solid commitment to being fully aware and conscious all the time. Being in the present is difficult for most of us today, especially since we have so many convenient distractions. Still, to improve your quality of life, becoming more heart-centered and reasonable in your daily interactions is vitally important.

Once you make the decision of how you wish to be and commit to making a change, the next thing to do is develop a way to stop yourself from heading into a reaction. This is when self-awareness is really important. For me, whenever I felt myself wanting to react in an area I wished to change, I would have a virtual "stop sign" pop up in my mind's eye.

An example of this occurred when I was raising my daughter. She was three years old and carrying a small glass of milk; she spilled it. *My* mother was a very reactionary kind of person. She would have been startled by the spilt milk and would have snapped at me about being clumsy. I had made a commitment to not be the same way with my daughter. When she spilled the milk, I had a strong feeling to react the way my mother had. But it didn't feel right, and the "stop sign" popped into my mind, accompanied by the words: "Don't be like Mom." I took a few deep breaths and said to myself, "She's only three." I quickly changed gears and instead of scolding my daughter, I reminded her how she had to practice being careful; then I showed her how to clean up the mess. There were no shouting, no tears, and my daughter learned that one has to be careful when carrying a glass of liquid.

People spill things, and it's okay. You just have to clean it up. I knew if I could continue to consciously respond in this way as she grew up, she would feel different about herself from the way I had. I was breaking a pattern of behavior, and hopefully she would learn to do the same when needed.

Habits are not always easy to change. As I mentioned before, it takes commitment and effort, at least at first. If you begin with a small change, then move to more complex relationships, it becomes easier to change from reaction to response. A client of mine was having difficulties with her marriage, family, and work. Moving from work mode to family and back was hard for her. She spent a lot of time in her car, on the phone for her work or taking her children to school and various activities. She was feeling frazzled and overwhelmed. So I asked her: "*How* do you wish to *be* when you are dealing with any of these issues?" It was not an easy question for her to answer, because she had never thought that she could change things by focusing on herself first. She told me that she wished to feel more secure, be less pressured by work and family issues, and enjoy life more.

Next I asked her to become aware of when she felt frazzled or overwhelmed. When she did, she needed to recognize the feelings, then give herself a moment to take a few deep breaths. I mentioned that if she was in the car and came to a stoplight, she could take the time to breathe and remind herself of how she "wishes to be." Then, from this "being present" space, to ask herself: "What could I choose to be my best response right now?" Sometimes, she would pull over and return a phone call. Mostly, she learned to let the situation go until she was in a better position to deal with it.

After a few weeks of just stopping, becoming aware and present, and remembering that she always has choice in how she responds at any given moment, her life changed dramatically. Slowly, she began to figure out what worked for her, what helped her keep a sense of calm in all situations. Most of the difficulties didn't go away, but how she responded to them changed. In many cases, the people around her began to alter how they handled situations as well, because they were picking up on her new sense of calm and happiness; her relationships began to run more smoothly. Situations where she couldn't adapt her responses didn't overwhelm her as they used to do, because she now saw them with a different perspective.

In our life experiences, we deal with all sorts of issues. Some days we may even feel bombarded by them. However, we always have a choice in how we respond. If we continue to react in the same ways, expecting things to change, we will only be disappointed again and again.

When in an unconscious state of mind, we expect the other person to change, and thus we see them as the problem. In reality, change can only come from within. So by changing from an unconscious reaction to a heart-centered response that is in line with how we wish to always be, we will change our relationship experiences and thus our life experiences. We become the best of who we are.

Debra L. Hanes is a certified professional coach and holistic theologian. From many years of personal experience and observation, she brings unique insights into her coaching practice as she guides her clients toward living with more authenticity. She also leads a weekly meditation group and a monthly book group called Spirituality Discussed.

For more information on Debra's coaching practice,
please visit www.thepathwaysforward.com.

# Homes Are Like Us ...
# They Respond Well to Love

## by Stephanie Bennett Vogt, MA

*How then do we "come home" spiritually and dwell
there? In my own life I have found no better way than
to value and savor the sacredness of daily living,
to rely on repetition, that humdrum rhythm, which
heals and steadies. Increasingly it is for me a matter
of being willing "to be in place," to enter into deeper
communion with the objects and actions of the day
and to allow them to commune with me. It is a way to
know and be known . . . to surrender my isolation by
participating in the experience as it happens.*

—Gunilla Norris, *Being Home*

When I read the preface to a wonderful little book called *Being Home,* by Gunilla Norris, I realized that my love of doing repetitive housekeeping tasks, like washing the dishes or putting away the same things in the same places every day, wasn't me just being hopelessly obsessive compulsive—as I might have believed (and my family might teasingly argue is the case).

Putting away is how I get centered. It connects me to a still place within myself. Folding laundry, sweeping the floor, clearing up the living room before I go to bed, or hanging the wash up to dry on a warm and sunny day (and smelling its freshness when I take it down) are ways that I slow down and quiet the mind. I am soothed and nourished by the ordinary—by what Norris calls "the extraordinary beauty of dailiness."

No matter what the task—whether it be fluffing up the pillows, gathering dirty cups and dishes, or turning out the lights before heading to bed—when I bring a quality of mindfulness to a simple chore, I notice that I *always* feel happier: calmer, lighter, freer. I also notice that my home responds to all of this, somehow, through me.

As a longtime professional space clearer, I've become intimately, and acutely, aware of the interconnectedness between humans and their homes; how the spaces we occupy respond to our attentiveness (or lack of it) and how they, in turn, reflect us, affect us, support us (and oppress us). Our homes are not just these big empty boxes that we fill with our collections of stuff, our life experiences, and our unique personalities. Seeing the way Western cultures treat and objectify their dwellings and their things, it's evident to me that most people have no idea how *alive* our living spaces really are.

It's our second skin; homes and workplaces are extensions of us. Through doorways and hallways, they circulate energy *(chi)*—or don't, depending on how cluttered, congested, and gummed up they are. Like people, they feel stress and get out of balance, even sick. They breathe by expanding and contracting. They are affected by the land they sit on, the neighboring properties, the physical contents and emotions of their occupants, and, yes, even the residue of happy and painful memories left behind by the previous residents. Homes thrive when they're nourished and well-tended. Like people, they respond well to love.

I once cleared a space for a client who was coming

out of a failed long-term marriage. She had just moved into an 1875 New England farmhouse and wanted her home to support a fresh start in her life. She hoped that I could release any energies that might negatively influence her, including the furniture she had purchased on Craigslist that might still be carrying the energetic residue of its previous owners.

Sure enough, as I approached her "new" master bed, I could feel waves of tears, contractedness, shallow breathing, and a hint of nausea coming from the side of the bed she did not sleep on (and unconsciously avoided). Because I knew that none of the emotional "off-gassing" was mine, I could bring the bed back into balance by simply being aware of the physical (and sometimes unpleasant) sensations arising through me and by *not identifying with any of them as my own*. Three minutes later, the bed felt clear and sparkling. Three months after our session, my client was gushing about the wonderful new man she had just met. In less than a year, she was thirty pounds lighter, in love, and living her dream.

I often tell my clients and students that space clearing is "loving up" a place; bringing our things and our thoughts, our loved ones and our living spaces back into balance by simply being a witnessing, compassionate presence. Watch a mother hold her disconsolate child without conditions or an agenda or a need to fix or "do" anything, and you get the idea. The child walks away, feeling all better because his mom simply held a space for him. Likewise, a simple act of mindful tending does wonders to shift the energy in a space.

You can practice this yourself by doing something in your home that makes *you* feel good. The good energy will ripple out and circulate into all areas of your home and life. If you like to cook, for example, prepare something that you love, a dish that creates fragrances that you know will waft and linger. If you like to dance or listen to music, crank up the music and boogie at least once a day . . . maybe even while you're cooking or washing the dishes.

Clap, rattle, ring a bell, or sing out loud to get the energy moving. Sweep the front steps. Clear a drawer or just *move* a pile from one location on the desk to another. Every day.

Change the sheets. Take a hot salt and soda bath or shower. Snuggle into your clean bed while breathing out an audible *ahhhhh*. Reframe a negative thought with a positive alternative. *"I'm late again"* could be *"I'm here, I made it!"* for example.

Laugh. Out loud. And if you can't bring yourself to feel good at any given moment, simply *allow that,* without trying to fix or change anything.

If you tune in and listen, you may just notice that your home will be humming right along with you.

STEPHANIE BENNETT VOGT, MA, is one of the world's leading space-clearing experts and the author of the award-winning *Your Spacious Self: Clear Your Clutter and Discover Who You Are.* She brings thirty-five years of experience to SpaceClear, a teaching and consulting practice she founded in 1996, which helps homes and their occupants come back into balance. Stephanie serves on the faculty of the New England School of Feng Shui and the Kripalu Center, and she writes and speaks internationally on personal clearing, simplifying, and cultivating what she calls "spacious detachment."

Learn more about Stephanie and her inspirational clearing programs at www.spaceclear.com.

# Take a Family Sabbatical

## by Lisa Merrai Labon

*The evidence of success is joy.*
—Abraham Hicks

I was sitting in an auditorium full of well-educated, highly polished, caring parents listening to another parent talk about why 80 percent of straight-A students cheat to maintain their grade-point averages. Denise Pope, founder of Challenge Success, a Stanford Education School project, asked the parents what they wanted for their children.

*Health, Education, Happiness.* We all nodded in approval. Yes. Yes. Yes.

"And yet," she said pausing dramatically, "when you ask the students what their parents want for them, what do you think *they* say?"

We scratched our heads and looked around the room for insights from our overachieving peers. I imagined my oldest daughter with her hands on hips, miming my words, "Clean your room, brush your hair, eat your veggies."

Pope continued, "They said that their parents want them to get straight As so they can go to the best colleges and universities; get a high-paying job so they can buy the big house and fancy car."

There it was. A truth so mundane and obvious, like the clutter we hide in closets or the stop signs we coast through. Our values, just like our laws, are constantly undermined by the reality of how we live. None of us in that auditorium was walking the talk.

Children learn what they live, and we are teaching our children that money and acquisition of stuff is the only thing that really matters. We demonstrate greed with our infinitely destructive consumption-driven economy. We demonstrate ignorance with the leveling of wild lands and habitats. We demonstrate cruelty with our approval and use of toxic chemicals and endless warfare on other humans and cultures.

Family is considered the primary place where values are taught and shared, yet "family face time" is almost nonexistent in many households. The typical American family watches thirty-six hours of television a week (per person) and rarely eats meals all together. Children aged eight to eighteen spend more than seven and a half hours a day on a device with a screen. Parents and children are lost in a bizarre technological prison disguised as progress.

We left that evening's presentation very uneasy. There had to be a better way to live, a better way to convey our values to our children. We wanted our children to make better decisions than we had. We wanted them to listen to their deepest desires, follow their talents and skills, and not be swayed by competitive peers or salary levels. We knew that time was running out for us, as our oldest child would be entering upper school in a couple of years and be off to college in the blink of an eye.

In 2008, our family decided to take a sabbatical. We did not have a concrete plan, which made it all very exciting and a bit terrifying. My husband left his longtime career as an investor. We left our coveted private schools. We sold our Pacific Heights home just as the real estate markets came crashing down. We sold or donated half a houseful of goods and said farewell to the rat race.

I began a blog called "Life on Purpose" to document our travels and challenges along the way. With homeschooling, we were able to live in a small fishing village in Sayulita, Mexico, as well as try out alpine life in Aspen, Colorado. The rest of the year, we explored areas of the Pacific Northwest. I wrote about the highs and lows, never sure where we would end up.

The main objective throughout our exploration was to find joy—in ourselves, in each other, in life. If nothing else, we wanted to walk the talk. No matter where it led us. We thought a lot about how we could strengthen our family through shared experiences, optimized health, growing our own food, and finding a community of likeminded souls.

Our year-long adventure was not without stress and strain. Our children were not used to having both parents focused on them 24/7. We had to set some serious ground rules and all adjust to sharing closer space. Traveling with small children is not easy, but homeschooling is wonderful, as long as you have cooperative children and local support. Some communities were more welcoming than others. And certainly travel can be expensive. I had hoped to continue our adventures for a few more years, going on to Australia and Europe, but I soon realized that the children and I needed to put down roots somewhere. So we began a family project to "find a new home."

After months of research and family discussions over delicious home-cooked meals, we found our home in Park City, Utah. It is a perfect combination of community, educational options, outdoor activities, and sun. We would not have found this amazing new way of life without taking a chance and breaking out of our routines.

Here are my tips to create your own family sabbatical:

**1. Start a savings account and plan your adventure.** There are so many ways to go. Research your likely options, from an RV adventure to a global tour. You will find that the choices are endless. I know families who have biked from Alaska to Argentina or sailed around the Caribbean for ten years. Whatever you do, make it bold. Step outside your comfort zone.

**2. Downsize and simplify.** Sell your stuff. Pare down to only what you really need. We had one bag each in Mexico, and it was more than enough. Get rid of the televisions, the toys, the heirloom furniture, the books (that was hard for me). The less you have to store or worry about housing, lugging, and tracking, the more money and freedom you'll have for your adventures.

**3. Rethink your work.** Consider your options; everything from taking leave, job sharing, working remotely, or even starting a whole new career. For inspiration on passive income or ways to automate your career, read Tim Ferriss's bestseller *The 4-Hour Work Week*. Also check out LocationIndependent.com for tons of ideas.

**4. Children are resilient!** I've heard parents say, "Oh, my kids would never want to leave their schools or friends." Do not use children as an excuse. Travel and shared experiences with family is a priceless, vital gift that only you can give them. Extended travel and cultural exchange is possibly the best experience anyone can ever have.

**5. The ultimate education.** Homeschooling is like the ultimate tailored education. Add journaling to your deluxe field trip, and your child will be miles ahead. There are hundreds of co-ops, charter schools, and homeschooling groups in every state and country. There are even homeschooling consultants to help you select the best curriculum. Rest easy; you will be offering your children an amazing opportunity.

A family sabbatical will enlighten, inspire, and motivate profound and often unexpected changes in your lives. It's wild, messy, and scary, but it also strips away the modern distractions and clutter so that one can finally see the abundant joy always available to us, no matter where we live. Whether you go for a month or many years, you will discover along the way a renewed definition of success and an enduring bond that will serve your children better than test scores or iPods.

Lisa Merrai Labon is a passionate advocate for healing local communities and the Earth as a whole. As a writer, Lisa has invited her readers to embrace their own lives with conscious intention by exploring community values, health, education, and spiritual connections. She lives with her family in Park City, Utah, and is working on her first novel.

Visit her website at about.me/lisamerrailabon.

# Redefining the
# Great American Ritual

## by Patricia Cohen

We the people have gathered in this great land of freedom, one that gives us the opportunity to make of our lives what we will. We are all citizens here, by our own decision or the wise decisions of our ancestors. Whether we migrated here, were brought here, were born here, or were native to this land before Columbus journeyed here, we are all a part of the past, the present, and the future of these United States. We are one people, under God, indivisible.

Regardless of where our families originated, there was an important culture from which we came.

This vast richness of our heritage, traditions, social networks, or family structure was often left behind, modified, or lost over time. A sense of sacredness of life and of the land we live in has been forgotten.

Because this is a country that is made up of the people and cultures of the world, we call ourselves the "melting pot." But we have melded into a country without a uniform formal practice for acknowledging growth and what is sacred.

Almost any culture from which we originated had traditions or rites of passage that symbolized the changing individual and strengthened his status in the family and community. What's required now is to rediscover those meaningful experiences and expectations that can empower us to be a part of the larger community and that remind us of the sacredness of life.

Rituals, ceremonies, and rites of passage can bond us with our families and neighborhoods more than just sharing a country.

It is interesting that we do not yet have a purely "American" custom that embraces all of us in the melting pot and serves as a defining rite of passage— or do we? Such a custom would benefit healthy growth for all ages and further strengthen and unite the diverse family that we are.

I suggest that an American ceremonial rite of passage has been right in front of us the whole time: the birthday celebration.

Birthday celebrations signify not only a bond between individuals and between families and communities, but they also showcase the development of the individual from infant to child to adult.

It is important to know that your contribution to your family and community is valued, and a birthday celebration is the perfect time to acknowledge that contribution.

The entire family helps to shape a child's being as she grows. Children are born as almost perfectly clean slates. A newborn child may have inherent gifts that can be developed, but the child cannot know what the rules of the family and the household are, how to succeed in school, how to be a functioning part of the community, or even how to care for herself. These are skills that are taught by the family as the child matures. Birthdays mark the points of additional freedoms and responsibilities for a child.

Recognizing the passage into full and late adulthood with birthday celebrations is just as important as when we were children. Once a member of the family becomes an adult, he knows what responsibilities are expected of him; the elder members of a family are honored and respected for their wisdom on this special day. All of these things are brought into the annual counting of the years that mark the milestones one has reached.

Incorporating and recognizing special accomplishments from the previous year, such as a new job, a marriage, or other life-changing event, will add to the rejoicing in birthday celebrations and can further unite and strengthen family and communal bonds. Recognizing our achievements at a birthday celebration adds an element of ritual that can have a profound effect on us and remind us that we are sacred.

Each family can make the ritual as simple or elegant as they wish. By adding rituals into your birthday celebrations, they are more easily recognized as the rites of passage that they are, and this is the best common denominator we all have in the great melting pot of cultures.

It's time to take our birthday celebrations to the next level, honoring them as the rites of passage and markers of growth for the individual that they are. In so doing, we can redefine this time of festivity as the great American ritual.

Patricia Cohen is a former president of the board of the Nevada County Jewish Community Center, vice president of the board of the Mariposa Waldorf School, and vice president of the board and program coordinator of New Frontiers of the Gold Country, a nonprofit educational organization. Her education in human development and working with children in the religious school, public school, day care center, and juvenile hall has given her a unique insight into the benefit of ritual and tradition as a tool for the unification of families.

In her book, *The Sacred American*, Patricia ventures beyond the mundane drudgery of day-to-day survival by offering meaningful solutions to the challenges of our time.

Visit her website at www.sacredamerican.com.

# Turning Coal into Diamonds

## by Craig Meriwether

There are times when life just doesn't go right. You struggle to keep it together but end up disappointed, hurt, angry, and depressed—an irrational mess. Life seems to be poking you with a sharp stick and getting a good laugh from doing so. These are the days when you're so overwhelmed that you feel discouraged and beaten down, ready to give up.

Yet what if there were a reason that problems keep showing up? It could be that these challenges are a gift, and all the hurt, pain, and failure is actually there to help you; perhaps your frustration, sadness, and anger can be used to build an amazing life of happiness and joy. This isn't some woo-woo pseudo philosophy. This is science, baby.

The second law of thermodynamics, or the law of entropy, describes how chaos naturally increases *in anything* until some outside energy is applied to reverse the process. For example, when you take a frying pan off the stove, the heat will spread out, and the pan will cool down unless you put it back on the burner.

In nature there is no standing still. Everything is either growing or dying, going forward or moving back.

People are the same way. Unless we are actively working on developing ourselves, applying energy to our lives, we gradually diminish and lose our skills. If we stay in our comfort zone and stop moving forward, then we have introduced the law of entropy into our lives. We're not growing; we're dying.

However, when Nobel Prize–winning scientist Ilya Prigogine was studying this phenomenon, he discovered something amazing. If you put a normal organism or compound in a closed environment and pass a small amount of energy into it, the energy will pass out again. Energy in, energy out, simple enough. As more and more energy is added, though, pressure builds, and the organism begins to overload. In other words, it becomes aggravated and irritated. This is the state of perturbation. I'm guessing that you might know what it feels like to be perturbed. By increasing the amount of energy and pressure, the organism shifts into chaos until it reaches a point at which it seems unable to handle any more. At the point of maximum overload, systems begin to fail; they start to decay and turn toward entropy—again, no big discovery.

But what Dr. Prigogine observed, and why he won the Nobel Prize, is that under the right conditions, something spectacular happens. Things do not fall apart; they do not blow up; they do not end in chaos. Instead, the organism will actually reorder itself, and it will evolve into a more complex structure. We can do the same thing. We can take the pressure and chaos of our lives and use it to move to a higher level. This is why some cancer patients will say—despite the horror and terror that is cancer, chemotherapy, and radiation—that it was the best thing that ever happened to them. They now live every day to the fullest, because they took that overwhelming chaos and reordered themselves to the next level. They had the option to become bitter and hostile toward life, but instead they chose to grow emotionally, mentally, and spiritually.

If things aren't going the way you want in your life, well maybe that's the point. The challenges and problems are showing up because you are ready to move to the next level. You have an amazing vision for your life. You created this vision with your hopes, dreams, and wishes, but you're unable to grasp hold of it just yet. The Universe heard you, however, and has composed a symphony of circumstances and situations so that you may grow emotionally, mentally, and spiritually—if you choose. The Universe will provide you with the right pressure and stress for you to reorder yourself and move to a higher level.

*But* . . . this will only happen under the right conditions. The right conditions exist when you support yourself mentally and emotionally in a healthy, positive, and enlightened manner. It is only when your thinking and mental programming can anchor you in any storm that you will be able to reach the next level.

You see, your depression, anger, limiting beliefs, unwanted emotions, outdated programs, conflicts, frustrations, and stress are keeping you from being something very important: resourceful.

"Resourceful: once again, full of source." Nowadays, "source" is defined as "where all things originate." But this wasn't the definition long ago. A mentor of mine, Jim Britt, the author of *Rings of Truth*, discovered the true definition in a five hundred-year-old dictionary at a London antiques store. In that dictionary, "source" was defined by one word: *love*. So the real definition of "resourceful" is: "once again full of love, where all things originate." Change can only occur if you are in a resourceful environment on the inside, if you are full of love. But if you are holding on to old anger, sorrow, and negative beliefs, you cannot move to the next level.

It was Albert Einstein who said, "You cannot solve a problem from the same consciousness that created it. You must learn to see the world anew." In other words, you cannot create your new life with the same mindset that created the life you have now. As Wayne Dyer so aptly put it, "When you change the way you look at things, the things you look at will change."

Within you right now are all the raw materials required for you to create extraordinary diamonds from the coal in your life. You *can* live in peace and happiness, but you have got to stop walking the path of fear and struggle. You must choose to become *resourceful*—once again full of love.

So here is your work. You must find a method or, better yet, several methods for creating a resourceful space within you. Some options are meditation, yoga, cognitive behavioral therapy, or emotional releasing techniques, such as the Sedona Method, EFT, or the releasing work I teach. You need to find some way to remove your stuck emotions, applying whichever approach works best for you, and use it on a *daily* basis. By resourcefully allowing the pressure and stress in your life to break through to the other side, you will reorder your life and you will shine, giving a whole new meaning to: "What doesn't kill me will make me stronger"—as strong as diamonds.

CRAIG MERIWETHER struggled with depression for more than twenty-five years. Then he discovered how to turn that intense emotional pain into "diamonds." He teaches his insights and ideas for awakening to real happiness and creating diamonds through a free online video course at his website www.CraigInRealLife.com. Craig is also the creator of the forthcoming breakthrough program "Depression 180—Turn It Around: How to End Depression, Anxiety, Self-Hatred, and Create Lasting Happiness!"

You can learn more about it at www.Depression180.com.

# Stop, Reverse, and Celebrate!

## by Marcelle Charrois

When I started school, I was confronted by the realization that my name, Marcelle, was unusual for the English-speaking majority population of our little Canadian town. We were part of a small and close-knit French community, which was regularly immersed in the language and culture of the Anglophone majority, as well as the nearby influences of the United States just across the border. "Marcelle, that's a boy's name," the kids in the schoolyard would often tease. As for any child, this kind of mockery really hurt. I remember coming home one day with tears streaming down my face. As I walked through the door, I exclaimed to my mother: "Mom, why did you give me such a name?"

My mother calmly responded by recounting the story of how my name was decided upon. Prior to having me, she had a miscarriage. While in the hospital, she was very lonely, as my father could only visit in the evening when he returned from work. My mother could not talk with the nursing staff because she could only speak French, and they spoke English. Fortunately, she found solace with a very sweet fifteen-year-old French girl who had had her appendix removed. The girl's name was Marcelle. In appreciation for Marcelle's daily visits, my mother promised her that the next child she would have, boy or girl, would bear her name.

Upon hearing this story, a significant shift occurred within me. My name was the fruit of the love and caring consideration of a young fifteen-year-old girl. Now that was special!

So what was I to do the next time someone at school or elsewhere mocked or questioned my name? I carefully considered my options as I vowed that my name must no longer be the target of ridicule but be recognized for its true value and worth!

The next time my name became the subject of

scrutiny, in a joking manner I announced: "Well, you must understand, I am from the planet Mars; so that's where my name comes from." Much to my surprise, the response was quite favorable! People laughed and joked back with me. Some of them even started to joyfully greet me using such names as "Mars Bar" in a show of acceptance and acknowledgment of my uniqueness.

Wow! What a discovery I had made. By shifting my response, I had created a whole new realm of possibility. Right then and there, a new life emerged, and, over the years, the stories I told of my Martian origins continued to be told and to evolve. To this day, it still strikes a positive chord with the people I meet.

What was it about what I did that essentially changed everything? The answer to that question lies within a thought-, action-, and result-shifting process that I refer to as Stop, Reverse, and Celebrate (SRC)!

Think back to a time in your life when you felt like "the odd man out" or when things really weren't going your way. Do similar feelings of *"alienation"* or frustration haunt you today?

The good news is that there is a way to completely redefine those experiences. A way to reconnect with the irrefutable truth that shouts out: "You are beautiful!" Your unique make-up and experiences have shaped you into the person that you are meant to be and continue to become. In fact, you have much to offer this world, just as you are, at any given moment in your life.

When past or present experiences elicit feelings that are not in alignment with who you really are and where you wish to be in your life, here are three simple steps, with accompanying questions, that will help you reconnect with the irrefutable truth that you are beautiful and perfect exactly the way you are:

1. **Stop (S):** What am I feeling? What triggered those feelings? What learning can I draw from this?

2. **Reverse (R):** Is this really about me? Instead, what do I choose to believe about myself? What am I grateful for? What do I wish to create more of in my life starting now? What can I think, feel, and do differently to produce better results?

3. **Celebrate (C):** How can I validate and celebrate with concrete actions the truth that has just been revealed by these questions and answers?

Make a commitment now to connect with your beautiful self by drawing upon the SRC-shifting process every day. By stepping into it with both feet, you will be able to positively shift your responses to seemingly negative experiences and realize that you are beautiful and perfect exactly as you are. Your destiny awaits you with the richness and fullness of all the colors of the rainbow!

MARCELLE CHARROIS is a heart intelligence coach, and as such, she draws upon her wide-ranging background and experience with yoga, meditation, metaphysics, and natural healing practices to help people create their best life today! Her first book, *The Alien in Your Closet: Open the Door to Your Inner Child and Unleash Your True Destiny!,* empowers people to reconnect with their intuitive instincts, true identity, and passion while actively reversing the undesirable effects of social conditioning.

For more information, please visit
www.True2HeartLiving.com.

# Quantum Soul Clearing: Three Steps to Transform Your Life

## by Michelle Manning-Kogler

Whether we like it or not, our thoughts and feelings are intricately tied to one another. Like a top that spins around and around, our recurring thoughts and beliefs can trigger feelings that keep us stuck in self-defeating behaviors and blind us to the answers that we need for change. These self-defeating patterns of thinking and feeling amount to what I call "negative energetic charges." To compound the situation, these negative energetic charges result in our brains making neural connections that lock those unhelpful thoughts and feelings into place. They hardwire the brain and the body for a conditioned expectation and outcome. That is why the same things seem to happen to us over and over again—and why it is so difficult to make changes in our lives.

My Quantum Soul Clearing Process is the result of years of research in energy medicine, distance energy healing, quantum physics, quantum mechanics, string theory, psychology, and brain research. It combines spiritual truths with cutting-edge scientific discoveries to effect profound changes. The process is a simple three-step method that removes the negative energetic charges you may be feeling toward other people, past events, current events, or yourself. With this healing method, you have the power to change how you feel about anyone or anything in just moments.

By using this process, you can give yourself peace of mind and raise your self-esteem and self-confidence. This confidence boost will enable you to know that you will succeed in whatever you choose to do, which can help you to make more money or heal your body. You will be able to reinvent yourself by removing the barriers and struggles from your life.

The first step in the process is learning how to

connect within, to the place where your Highest Self resides. I call that place "Divine Core Center." It is usually located near the diaphragm beneath the ribs, and it feels like the core or center of your body. This is often where you'll feel "gut reactions" and intuitive whispers from Source. That is because it is the place where that spark of God, or Source, resides within each of us!

Once you have located your Divine Core Center, the next step is to use a specific set of clearing statements that can systematically remove these negative energetic charges from your physical body, your energy bodies, your soul, and every aspect of your being. The energetic blocks usually have deep roots in generational programming, societal training, and are held in the collective beliefs of humanity. Those thoughts and feelings may even be embedded in our environments and throughout time and space. By clearing these negative energies, with the specific statements, you deactivate them and any influence they may have had on you.

Once the negative energetic charges are completely resolved, the final step of the process begins. This is where you work with your Highest Self to download and replace the cleared negative thoughts and experiences with your desires. This is when you get to design your life exactly the way you want it to be.

For example, let's say you were trying to get over a betrayal by your spouse and the unpleasant divorce that followed. Every time you think about your ex-husband or ex-wife, you feel hurt and angry. You may feel like you weren't special enough or good-looking enough or worthy enough to keep him or her interested in you. This may trigger feelings of low self-esteem, self-judgment, self-hatred, or other negative emotions. You want to get over all of it but just can't seem to move on.

To work with the Quantum Soul Clearing Statements, the first thing to do is focus your attention within the Divine Core Center and connect to your Highest Self. Ask your Highest Self to create a safe space in which you can work and clear. Make it your intent to work with your Highest Self to release the problem.

Then you would say the following clearing statement out loud: "Clear the betrayal and everything it represents throughout my body, my energy bodies, and *me;* all my systems; my ego and all its systems; my mitochondria, all their generations, and all their systems; all my generations and all of their systems; my proteins, environments, associations, and entanglements; my personal and collective consciousness, subconsciousness, and unconsciousness; all personal, planetary, and universal Core Operating Systems; and all my interfaces and connections to all those systems and how they affect me in any way, shape, form, time, place, or space, at all levels, layers, and depths of my being." Make this statement with full intensity, and as you do, you will feel the energetic charge completely dissipate and dissolve throughout your entire body!

Each time you recite the clearing statement, you are effectively asking for that energy to be removed from you; you are asking to break resonance with the frequency; and you are asking that the habit or addiction to the negative frequency be completely removed.

As a final step, after the full clearing statement has been completed, ask for a download of the frequencies of feelings you desire that can replace the frequency of betrayal. You might ask for things such as love, honesty, right relationships, joy, healing, peace, peace of mind, compassion, trust, wholeness, caring, being cherished, self-respect, respect from others, fidelity, honor, or integrity. Ask for everything you want until you can't think of anything else.

As you ask for all these positive frequencies to be downloaded to you, you will actually feel yourself begin to get lighter and lighter, more joyful and happier than you've felt for a very long time. You will feel an overwhelming sense of relief and a feeling of being unburdened. We are meant to feel joyful!

You may also have to clear other energies, such as anger, frustration, low self-esteem, unworthiness, self-judgment, judgment of others—and anything else that comes up regarding the situation—to completely heal from the divorce.

This is a process of learning to be the master of your experiences and, ultimately, to take charge of your life and your creations. You get to choose how you feel and how you react to situations. You get to choose exactly what it is that you want to experience. You no longer have to feel like you are victimized or a passive participant in your life. In the process, you will find peace of mind, a deeper connection with Source, and a sense of true Self that you've never experienced before.

MICHELLE MANNING-KOGLER is the author of *Quantum Soul Clearing: Your Ultimate Guide to Personal Transformation.* She is a life coach, distance energy healer, medical intuitive, bio-energetic practitioner, and motivational speaker. She is the developer and trainer for "The Quantum Soul Clearing Process."

Michelle has overcome a devastating diagnosis of rheumatoid arthritis. From that experience and years of extensive education and training, she has created customized whole-life health and wellness programs to help others achieve their optimal health goals.

She lives in Utah with her husband and two cats.

Visit her website at www.quantumsoulclearing.com.

# The Golden Rule:
# A Universal Axiom

## by Rev. Stacy Goforth

The "Golden Rule" that many people grew up with is: "Do unto others what you would have others do unto you." It's widely thought that this is a Christian teaching, but it's actually a fundamental teaching of many faiths. For example:

**Baha'i Faith:** And if thine eyes be turned towards justice, choose thou for thy neighbor that which thou choosest for thyself. (Baha'u'llah, *Gleanings*)

**Buddhism:** Treat not others in ways that you yourself would find hurtful. (The Buddha, Udanavarga 5.18)

**Christianity:** In everything you do, do to others as you would have them do to you; for this is the law and the prophets. (Jesus, Matthew 7:12)

**Confucianism:** One word which sums up the basis of all good conduct . . . loving kindness. Do not do to others what you do not want done to yourself. (Confucius, Analects 15:23)

**Hinduism:** This is the sum of duty: do not do to others what would cause pain if done to you. (Mahabharata 5:1517)

**Humanism:** Humanists acknowledge human interdependence, the need for mutual respect, and the kinship of all humanity. (#5, Twelve Principles of Humanism)

**Islam:** Not one of you truly believes until you wish for others what you wish for yourself. (The Prophet Muhammed, Hadith)

**Jainism:** One should treat all creatures in the world as one would like to be treated. (Mahavira, Sutrakritanga)

**Judaism:** What is hateful to you, do not do to your neighbor. This is the whole Torah; all the rest is commentary. (Hillel, Talmud, Shabbath 31a)

**Native American Spirituality:** All things are our

relatives; what we do to everything, we do to our-selves. All is really One. (Black Elk)

**Shinto:** The heart of the person before you is a mirror. See there your own form. (Shinto saying)

**Sikhism:** I am a stranger to no one; and no one is a stranger to me. Indeed, I am a friend to all. (Guru Granth Sahib, p. 1299)

**Taoism:** Regard your neighbor's gain as your own gain, and regard your neighbor's loss as your own loss. (Lao Tsu)

**Wicca:** An harm it none, do as ye will. (Wiccan Rede)

**Zoroastrianism:** Whatever is disagreeable to yourself, do not do unto others. (Shayest na-Shayest 13:29)

It was through studying other faiths that I began to see the universality of the Golden Rule and began to apply it to my own interactions with others. When we take this rule to heart and we really start to live by it, it creates the opportunity for an unimaginable peace in our relationships with others.

So often, even when our intentions are good, we fall short of truly living out this rule. Because we don't know strangers or what they believe, we are likely to have an underlying fear of reaching out and helping them. They may think that we are trying to push our faith onto them. We might even fear that they could react aggressively. This fear makes us hesitate and hold back in our interactions with others. So to truly practice the Golden Rule, we must first overcome our fear.

The first step to applying the Golden Rule and relinquishing our fear is also perhaps the hardest: see other people as not so different from ourselves. We must recognize the humanity in everyone and in ourselves, too. We have a very deep something in common with every other person on the planet, whether we like them or not. Every person has a story. Stop for a moment to consider the person waiting in line in front of you at the grocery store. His, or her, life is like yours. Like you, he is tired at the end of a long day and realizes while in line that he has forgotten to get the milk. Or maybe she is struggling to get home in time to make dinner and is being distracted by a fussy child. These people are not so different from you. When it comes to the big things in life, we are more alike than different.

Now that you can see this person at the grocery store as someone who is not so very different from you (You're both buying groceries, right?), perhaps you can then think about what you can do that might make that person's day a little better. You could offer to run back to the dairy section to pick up the forgotten milk or hold his place in line while he goes to get it. You could produce the needed change for her, so she doesn't have to juggle both the toddler and her purse to find it. You could even just say hello and smile. This is what it means to love one another and treat others as we wish to be treated.

To break the cycle of fear of others, we just need to realize that all of us want the same things: to be happy, to experience peace, to feel love. The fact that all the major religions of the earth, as well as people who don't have any particular faith or don't even believe in God, still share the Golden Rule is evidence of this. The wording is slightly different, but you can see the common thread.

So often, we allow the differences in our religious beliefs to get in the way of how we see others. We may think—or even have been taught—that people of other faiths believe different things and can't be trusted, so our actions toward others mirror those thoughts and teachings. But it becomes apparent when reading these various "golden rules" that all faiths teach that we must love one another. It is incredible that we all have this beautiful rule in common. This simple teaching is a cornerstone of all the major religions and throughout humanity. It is apparent that we are meant to love each other.

It is important to remember this when interacting with other people, as it enables us to truly apply the Golden Rule. When we relate to others on the basis of our commonalities rather than differences, we are led to beautiful, deep, and meaningful relationships.

When we treat others the way we desire to be treated, it generates an energetic bond between us that allows them to interact with us in the same way. The nonverbal messages we send out to others are reflected to us by the way others treat us. When we interact with others from a basis of commonality and love, those feelings are reciprocated tenfold. We get back more love, more openness, and more understanding than what we give. What a beautiful way to live our lives!

Rev. Stacy Goforth's mission is to help educate people everywhere to the similarities of all faiths, increase understanding, and decrease fear and hatred.

She attended The New Seminary in New York City, was ordained as an Interfaith Minister in June 2011, and serves as an Associate Minister for the Interfaith Temple in New York City.

Stacy has served as editor for the *Creative Secretary's Letter* and *The Essential Assistant* professional newsletters published by the Bureau of Business Practices. She has been an editor for several additional newsletters and has written numerous articles for these and other publications.

Stacy and her husband, Bob, live in Groton, Connecticut and enjoy camping, kayaking, and hiking.

# An Attitude of Gratitude: The Gateway to Awakening

## by Jacob Nordby

I invite you to take a little journey of imagination with me. Imagine that you are driving down the road. You're in a hurry—late for an appointment. The traffic light turns yellow, but, two cars ahead, some cautious driver stops.

You thump your steering wheel in frustration. "Come on," you yell, "I have places to go!"

Fuming at the delay, you glance left and see a homeless man standing on the corner with his sign. He bends down and smiles at you, but you shake your head and wave him off. He steps closer, pulls something from his pocket, and taps on your window. Alarm squeezes your throat and you whip your head around, looking for an escape route. He taps again, and you look back. He's still smiling and now holds up a folded slip of paper.

"I'm supposed to give this to you," he calls through the glass.

Dubious, but hoping he'll go away if you comply, you buzz the window down a few inches, and he pushes the note through so that you can take it.

"Have a good day," he says with a smile.

A little amazed at what you just did, taking a note from a stranger, you have an intense, deep-seated feeling that something big just happened. You unfold the note. There is only one sentence on the paper, neatly written in blue ink:

"The greatest gift you can offer the planet is to awaken and walk in love."

Heart pounding at the strangeness of the situation, you take a deep breath and look around; you have received a special message from an unlikely messenger, one that could change your life.

Many people look around at the problems of the planet and feel powerless to make a difference. They are sure they can't do much to improve their own situations—much less solve the ages-old tangles of world hunger and disease and oppression. But if the imaginary letter in your hand right now were real, you could awake and walk in love.

Here's how the dictionary defines the word "awaken":

*Awaken: (verb) to wake up; to stir; to rouse from sleep; to spring into being.*

Your little note's message is beautiful because it doesn't require anything more than a shift in awareness. You don't need to suddenly become rich, beautiful, famous, or highly educated. All that's required is that you wake up and realize Who You Really Are—a unique, powerful expression of the Loving Source. Open your eyes and understand your role as a co-creator of a whole new experience on this planet. No obstacle can block the doorway to your awakening.

Perhaps you're thinking, "Well, that sounds nice, but I have no idea where to start."

I recommend a diet of pure gratitude. Start by observing everything in your life that is working. Give thanks for the eyes that are reading these words—they're truly amazing. Praise the breath in your lungs—a miracle happens every time you draw air into your body. Send a mental love note to your faithful heart, which beats more than one hundred thousand times per day whether you notice it or not. Without moving from your chair, you've already shifted your awareness! The same divine electricity that runs through your body also powers the stars in their eternal journey across the cosmos. In a flash of splendid appreciation, you have tapped that very energy for conscious use in your life now.

When you leave your house, give thanks for everything you see. Give thanks for the trees, the sky, the sun, and moon; even give thanks for the traffic jam.

And as this process unfolds, you will watch as the world transforms itself around you. Enjoy your new heaven on earth, and if you cross paths with someone who has fallen down, reach out your hand to help them up.

As you learn to walk and see in new ways, be gentle with yourself. Be kind to the tangled places and shower them with love. There are probably many puzzles in your life that will require time before they arrange themselves in a visible order.

As Rainer Maria Rilke once said: "Be patient

toward all that is unsolved in your heart and try to love the questions themselves."

The greatest gift you can offer the planet is to awaken and walk in love. With each step you take into a more loving life, you send vibrations throughout the web of consciousness. Everyone is affected when you become aware of your own perfect wholeness. There's no need to fight evil with the old weapons of hatred and anger. Those tools are worn out, and we are asked to pick up new instruments of peace.

Be assured, wherever you find yourself on this journey of awakening, you're not alone. Around the globe, people are receiving their own wakeup notes. You are joined by a growing multitude of peace mongers. So go ahead, allow the candle of your passion to burn hot again. The light you shine will attract those who are also bursting into flame. They will come near and assist as you give birth to your highest purpose.

Jacob Nordby is an author, speaker, and the founder of a popular spiritual web-magazine site, www.YourAwakened Self.com. He does personal coaching work with people who are moving through transitions in life.

# Finding Your Own Way:
# The Ultimate Quest

## by Tim Anstett

*I don't seek, I find*

—Pablo Picasso

In the legend of King Arthur, the knights of the roundtable undertake a sacred quest to find the Holy Grail. At a critical point in the tale, it's said that "each knight entered the woods where it was darkest" in his effort to complete the mission. This often-overlooked sentence is a powerful and telling metaphor. In the pursuit of something sacred, there comes a point in every quest at which we have to go it alone, forging ahead into the black and foreboding unknown, along no previously hewn or trampled path.

This is how mythology presents the pursuit of anything that is holy: the individual goes in alone, confronts the scariest of places, and must blaze his or her own trail. The message here is clear: It is only in going on one's own path that one is ever going to find that special thing, that feeling, that would clarify all of life.

Yet so many of us look for self-fulfillment in life by following the path of another. We mistakenly think that someone else has the ultimate and final answer for us. It is tempting and deceptively easy to let someone else do the finding for us, but it's my experience that strictly following the path of another will not yield the ultimate prize.

As for me, I walk and walk, always searching for the sacred, forever dipping into some religion or philosophy or psychology for a diamond in the rough that can explain or deepen my thoughts and feelings. I love all the choices these other paths offer, but I don't think that any one path will have all the answers for *me*. I study such things because I want to learn. I want to gain something different or new. In doing so, I make it my own.

As a result, I take a little of what Lao Tzu offers of the Three Treasures, what Nietzsche offers of *amor fati,* and on and on from Goethe and Albert Ellis and Buddha and more, until I have something that feels real and solid and applicable to me. Finding everything I need and want in one religion or philosophy is like only shopping in one store forever: a tad boring, to begin with, and some of the things I get just don't suit me. I can't imagine it fulfilling me. I don't believe that taking one part of Mohammad or Freud means I have to take the whole of what each offers. Then, when I mix all this together, I discover that I am making my own way, and for me, that's the only way to go.

Let me be clear, I am not denigrating a single path. Many have significant value, and for much of one's life, a single path can serve very well. But your life will not perfectly mirror the founder of your pre-worn path. So, at some point in your quest, you are going to have to deviate. You can choose to walk on Lao Tzu's road, for instance, but somewhere along the way you're going to face a crucial choice, a golden opportunity. I hope you won't be afraid to plunge into the woods at its darkest point and, in so doing, chart your own path to find what is sacred to you.

TIM ANSTETT is a life and work guide and the founder and principal of Three Treasures Tao Coaching. His first play, produced when he was twenty-two, was termed "chilling and lyrical" by the *Philadelphia Inquirer;* from there, he went on to write a dozen more plays, five novels, and *Honorable Work* (Lindisfarne Press, 1999), his first foray into nonfiction self-help. This book was also the culmination of Tim's eighteen years co-leading Success Training In Vocal Expression—or STRIVE, Inc.—a corporate-training firm that served more than four dozen Fortune 500 companies.

Over his life, he has worked with Academy Award–winning actors and convicted murderers, executives and the developmentally disabled, business owners and busboys, men and women, the wealthy and the homeless, and myriad others. He currently facilitates three to five personal-growth groups a year as the groups coordinator for Victories of the Heart, a men's organization, and is a high school boys' basketball coach.

# Helping Others Helps You

## by Randy Davila

*His Holiness the Dalai Lama describes two kinds
of selfish people—the wise and the unwise. Unwise
selfish people only think of themselves—and the result
is confusion and pain. Wise selfish people know that
the best thing they can do for themselves is to be there
for others. As a result, they experience joy.*

—Pema Chodron, *When Things Fall Apart*

In the summer of 2004, my friend Lydia Monroe journeyed to the African country of Kenya, on the eastern coast of the continent. As an American business woman in her late forties, traveling with a church group, nothing could have prepared Lydia for what she was about to witness.

While visiting the small town of Kitale, Lydia got a close-up look at some of Kenya's so-called "street children," a label given to the thousands of children orphaned by war, famine, disease, and neglect who wander aimlessly throughout the country, forced to beg, steal, and do whatever else it takes to survive.

On the same day that she had this experience, Lydia met Geoffrey Okumu, a young African man who, although trained as a social worker, was currently operating a small book store. In hindsight, this meeting would prove to be quite synchronistic.

Although her trip to Kenya was a brief two weeks, Lydia was touched at the deepest of levels and knew that she must do *something* to help the street children. No matter how big or small and no matter what the cost, Lydia felt compelled to act.

Upon her return to the United States, she began an email correspondence with Geoffrey about ways in which they could join forces to help as many of these children as they could. Shortly thereafter, an inspirational idea was born.

With Lydia's business experience and Geoffrey's

training as a social worker, they opened a small safe house in Kitale, appropriately named "Oasis of Hope." Fifty street children showed up on the first day to be fed, bathed, and loved. In the years since, Oasis of Hope has grown to serve 150 of Kenya's abandoned children, enrolling them in school, providing them with housing, and, most importantly, showing them love after they had experienced none.

All of this occurred because of one trip, one experience, and one divinely inspired desire: to help others in need.

As the CEO of Hierophant Publishing (the publisher of this volume), I am exposed to a wide variety of spiritual and self-help books that offer wisdom and instruction on how to live more vibrant and fulfilling lives. Ideas that encourage prayer, meditation, self-inventory, positive thinking, and the like are wonderful opportunities to further our understanding of ourselves and live the life of our dreams. I believe that practices such as these are indispensable.

At the same time, I think the most often forgotten and overlooked method of self-help is to *go out and help someone else.*

That's right, in addition to the obvious assistance

you are providing to someone in need, helping someone else also helps you. Why? It's simple. You feel good when you do it.

Helping others gets us out of our own self, and that's another benefit. When we help others, it brings balance to our perspective. Without this vocation, otherwise well-intentioned self-help practices can quickly turn into self-obsession practices. If we are stuck in the quagmire of our own self-inventory, our thoughts become consumed with "me, me, me," and we fail to remember that we are not alone on this planet, and that there are other human beings in far worse life situations than our own.

Also, it's often when we are feeling stuck in life, when we think things aren't going our way, that we can feel better simply by turning our attention to the needs of others. Try it; I think the results may surprise you.

The ways in which we can help are innumerable, and in my experience, we won't have far to look. Whether it's at work, in our neighborhood, or in our own family, I assure you that many opportunities to help others will arise when you begin to look for them.

One caveat to remember: occasionally I will hear

someone say, "I would help, but the problem is just too big; I couldn't possibly make a difference." If you hear yourself make that statement, please recognize it as another example of the ego's attempt to keep you trapped in the dungeon of despair, feeling powerless and stuck where you are.

Thankfully, Lydia and Geoffrey didn't fall for that one. And while their example is noble, courageous, and monumental, affecting the lives of hundreds of children in Kitale, Kenya, the real lesson is that by consciously helping others, we make the world a better place *and* make ourselves feel good, too.

RANDY DAVILA graduated with distinction from the Classics, Philosophy, and Religion Department at the University of Mary Washington in Fredericksburg, Virginia. He is the CEO of Hierophant Publishing and author of *The Gnostic Mystery*.

For more information, please visit
his website at www.randydavila.com.

For more information about Oasis of Hope, or to donate, please visit www.oasisofhopekitale.blogspot.com.

# Notes

## Creativity: The Recipe for Awakening

1. Thacher Hurd and John Cassidy, *Watercolor for the Artistically Undiscovered* (Palo Alto, CA: Klutz Publishing 1992).

## Relaxed Intention: A Pathway to Peace

1. Terrence Webster-Doyle, *Karate: The Art of Empty Self* (Ojai, CA: Atrium Publications, 1989).

## Be Happy and Success Will Follow

1. "Purpose," Positive Emotions and Psychophysiology Lab, University of North Carolina, Chapel Hill, www.unc .edu/peplab.

2. "Dynamic spread of happiness in a large social network: longitudinal analysis over 20 years in the Framing-ham Heart Study," James H. Fowler, Nicholas A. Christakis, University of California, Davis, http://jhfowler.ucsd.edu/ dynamic_spread_of_happiness.pdf, 2008.

3. Martin E. P. Seligman, PhD, *Authentic Happiness,* (New York: The Free Press, 2002).

Hierophant Publishing
8301 Broadway, Suite 219
San Antonio, TX 78209
www.hierophantpublishing.com
staff@hierophantpublishing.com
www.pearlsofwisdomthebook.com